PREDICAMENTS:

Mostly True

HUNTING & FISHING STORIES

 BY RANDY WILLIAMS

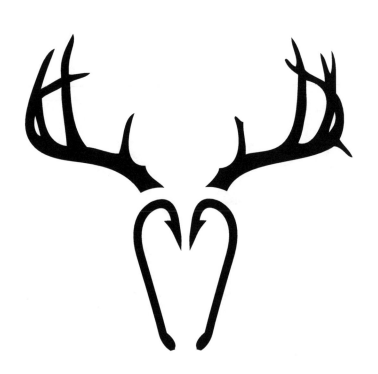

PREDICAMENTS:

Mostly True

HUNTING & FISHING STORIES

 BY RANDY WILLIAMS

This book is a work of fiction based on
true hunting and fishing experiences.

Predicaments: Mostly True
Hunting & Fishing Stories
Copyright © 2014 Randy Williams

Randy Williams
www.wilfish.com
williams2055@yahoo.com

Let's go fishing!

Graphic design and illustration by
Shawn Brook Williams
www.shawnbrookwilliams.com

1st Printing: January 2014
Printed by Createspace

Contents

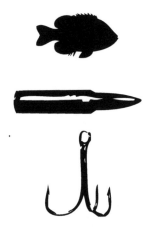

"It's a dandy, Randy!"

— *Robert Williams*

Foreword

Neatness and being prepared (even though I was a Boy Scout) is not particularly essential in my life. Unaware and jumping in with both feet is more my style. This existence would get anyone into predicaments. It leads one into a life of unpredictable exhilaration and spur-of-the-moment challenges, albeit some awkward and embarrassing situations. Luck or good friends have saved me so far.

That, by the way, is a fancy way of saying I can fall into a crap house but usually come out smelling like a rose. And that rose has a horseshoe stuck on its stem for the vase.

"It isn't that big fish that you caught; or that big buck you got hanging on the wall... it's the memories and adventures that will be the biggest trophy of all..."

— *Dale Littleton*
{theme to No Excuses tv show}

EIGHT POUNDS & SCREAMING

Here is an example of a bad situation turning out great. A friend convinced me to take his friend fishing (in this story names are withheld to protect the guilty). This guy was in his third day of trying to quit smoking. I was unaware how uncomfortable it could be to fish with or even be in the vicinity of a person a couple days into their cigarette withdrawal symptoms.

Even though largemouth bass were biting like crazy, after less than an hour he was ready to quit fishing. It does not sit easy with a fisherman to suspend a fishing trip when the fish are biting for any reason, let alone orneriness. I persuaded him to stick it out just a bit longer because there was one last place we needed to try. Even though it meant I would have to suffer a bit more of his naggingly bitter, nicotine-deprived behavior.

We eased the boat around the end of a sandbar that has produced several nice largemouth bass over the years. There was a tiny pocket where a row of arrowhead weeds met along the side of a patch of lily pads. There was also a small clump of bullrushes mixed in to make it the perfect place to catch a big bass. I tried to explain to this guy what a great spot this was and that he should place a cast right next to that tiny clump of bullrushes.

He made one poor halfhearted attempt at casting his lure into the spot and then proclaimed, *"It's time to go right now, the fish are not biting, and I might get more aggravated by mosquitoes if we stay."* I can't remember if it really was mosquitoes he mentioned or not, but there were so many things that bothered this guy I could not keep them straight.

And he was right about one thing it was time to go. If we left, we could end the misery for both of us.

But I was stubborn enough to attempt just one more cast. I wanted to show this guy that this was a great spot. My cast made a loud splash way off target. In fact, it landed at least six feet to the right of that perfect fish-holding spot. I guess I lowered my pole as I yelled, *"Darn it, I have had enough, let's go and get you back to shore!"*

Well, during the few moments it took to vocalize my frustration, the plastic worm I had on for a lure sank to the bottom. I started to wind it in, but there was pressure on the line. I set the hook and was yelling again, but this time it was joyous! An eight-pound largemouth bass splashed and fought before it succumbed to the landing net. In Wiscon-

sin, if it's eight-pounds it's a dandy. Or to borrow a quote my dad used when I was younger, "It's a dandy, Randy."

I entered that bass in the Lucky 13 fishing contest held in Eau Claire, Wisconsin. Because it was the largest bass caught for the entire year, I won a scoped 30-06 semi-automatic deer rifle. That fall I took the new rifle and shot a nice buck. I am a taxidermist, so I mounted that bass and won third place in the Wisconsin state taxidermy competition.

It takes a special ability to get into these kinds of predicaments and, fortunately for me, it's often good luck that follows.

I have wondered if that guy ever quit smoking for good. I hope so, even though his frustration directly resulted in my good fortune.

BAZOOKA BIRD

Jeff and I were going turkey hunting early one morning. It was the spring turkey season in Central Wisconsin.

As we parked at the edge of our hunting field, a heavy rain pelted the truck. We unloaded the gear and trudged across that slippery muddy field into the deluge. Often a rain like this would dampen your spirits, however I was too excited to let this rainstorm bother me.

Steve, the best Turkey Guru east of the Mississippi River, had scouted this field often, including yesterday. He assured us we would be covered in turkeys this morning especially if we did something that was unusual - at least unusual for me. He had hunted in that blind using decoys a few days before and discovered that the turkeys skirted around him and out of shotgun range. He correctly surmised that these birds were decoy shy. He told us to leave our turkey decoys at home.

After the long downhill walk across the slick field, we arrived at our hunting spot and found our turkey tent in the middle of a huge puddle of water. I was thinking the worst. We would not be able to hunt at our spot and would probably be stumbling around in the dark trying to find a dry place to hunt. But remember, even though Steve could not hunt that morning, he was watching out for us. He had checked the weather and anticipated the possibility of a puddle at our spot. We decided to check out the tent anyway. We sloshed across the water fumbling into the tent with all our gear. We were delighted to discover that Steve had the forethought to place a big heavy-duty mat under our tent the night before. It took a few minutes of scuffling around in the dark to set up the tippy little chairs, arrange the turkey calls, and adjust the camera. Steve's mat kept the chair's legs from oozing into the mud and that kept our butts out of the ever-growing puddle.

It is also important to arrange the tent windows so some are open enough to shoot through but not so wide as to allow the turkeys to see you. We hoped the turkeys would stay in their usual pattern and enter the field from the thick wooded roosting area on our left. We adjusted the tent windows for that scenario.

Jeff settled in his chair but because of his early wake up, along with the mesmerizing sound of rain caroming off our tent, Jeff fell asleep.

I double-checked everything and felt things were just about ready. (As if being ready for everything could actually happen while turkey hunting.) Because of the overcast sky it was barely light, but after another watch check, shooting time was now only 15 seconds away.

With the pounding rain it was noisy in the tent, but I thought I heard the sound of a bird landing just outside. It was hard to hear and also hard to believe a turkey could have made that noise. The season would be open in just a few seconds. Could it really have been a turkey already? As stated before, we had anticipated that if a turkey showed he would come in from the left. I peered out of the open window to the left, no bird. I had the same result after a glance out of the front window. There was however, a tiny hole to the right where the window flap was almost completely closed. I peered out of that small hole and got an adrenalin rush. There was not one, but *three* big long beard turkeys on the edge of the puddle *just outside of the tent.*

It was time to try and figure out a plan to pull off this shot. I managed to discreetly wake up Jeff because he should be in on the plan. With the birds that close, there was no way we could adjust the window flap to make it big enough to accommodate a gun and a camera. Surely, those keen turkey eyes would see the movement and spook. This meant we had to manage a camera and a gun without adjusting that small opening. The usual technique of holding the gun stock to my shoulder did not work because my head, when aiming down the sights, blocked the tent opening Jeff needed for his camera.

My next move was not the smartest move of the year. Fortunately or unfortunately, Jeff (who was intently looking through the viewfinder of the video camera) could not see the foolish plan I was contemplating. I actually placed the stock of the shotgun (which was loaded with 3½ inch magnum turkey loads) on top of my shoulder, bazooka style. Then, with my head slightly off to the side, I estimated the sight bead of the gun barrel at the turkey's neck. Strangely the thought of Tweety Bird from Warner Brothers cartoons now came into my consciousness. Tweety Bird would say "If I dood it I'll get a wippin." Well after a bit of angst Jeff finally got the camera focused on the birds and not the back of my head. When he said he had the bird in focus, "I dood it" and pulled the trigger. Wow did that hurt. The gun barrel reared back, hitting me in the face, and the butt of the stock, much to his surprise, slammed hard into Jeff's shoulder. The shotgun recoil knocked us both off our chairs and into the puddle of water we were sitting over.

After recovering from the sting of my stupidity, we slowly got back up out of the puddle, and peered out of that tiny hole. Believe it or not, we saw a turkey flopping on the ground. Jeff had filmed the turkey shot along with the

inside of the turkey tent he inadvertently filmed while lying on his back in the puddle. We gathered up our supplies, the soggy turkey, and then headed back to the truck.

After registering the bird, we were eating breakfast in a restaurant by 6:00 a.m. While drip-drying at the table, I held ice on my swollen cheek and Jeff rubbed his sore shoulder. Jeff had that Laurel and Hardy look on his face as if to say, "This is another fine mess you've gotten us into."

THE BEAR HUNT

Craig Cloutier and I decided to try a combination bear hunt/fishing trip in Canada. I had always wanted to get a bear and, hopefully, this would be my chance. We waded through several brochures, made a few calls, and randomly chose an outfitter. The plan for this trip was to fish during the day and hunt for bear in the evenings. After about a 12-hour drive, we arrived at Agnew Lake in Ontario, Canada. The first thing we did after unpacking was jump in the guide's boat. He gave us a tour of our immediate area around Spanish Lake and showed us all 16 bear bait stations. These stations had been baited with leftover meat scraps from butcher shops.

We backed our trailer into the landing to unload the boat and ready it to use for fishing and getting to our hunting stands. (Incidentally, I put a lock on my trailer to secure it to the hitch on Craig's truck. Unfortunately, I left the key to that lock at home.) Because of the missing key, we had to pull an empty boat trailer around behind Craig's truck every time we went somewhere. Getting into this sort of situation is typical for me.

Our guide mentioned to us that the more rancid the bait, the better the bears liked it. He had been gracious enough to leave a few bags of meat out in the hot sun for several days to ripen. This odorous bear delight was stored in a garbage can in my boat the whole trip. We kept it handy in case we came across a bear bait station that needed replenishing. This vessel of stench really added to the decor of my already cluttered boat.

All the bear baits are accessible by water only. The terrain is very rugged and traveling by water is the best way to get around this desolate area. On our tour of the area, the guide stated that no one had harvested a bear at this camp for two weeks. This was not an encouraging sign to start off our adventure. Fortunately, we discovered that bears had hit two baits, and our spirits were lifted with thoughts of big black bears ravaging our offerings.

That first evening, I chose the active stand that was farthest away from camp and used my boat to reach it. Craig chose the closer active stand and used the small 12-foot camp boat with the 5-hp motor to try and get there.

This spring bear hunt business does have a few drawbacks. As soon as you would get close to shore, especially in the evenings, hordes of mosquitoes and black flies swarmed you. They were buzzing around so thick that you could hardly even hear. Full body netting with leather gloves and duct tape around your ankles and wrists was the only salvation if you wanted to spend any unbitten time on a bear stand.

On the way to his stand, Craig had problems with the motor on the camp boat; rather than row all the way to the stand that had been hit by a bear (it was two miles away), he chose simply to row to the closest stand from camp. He pulled the boat up next to shore, tied the boat off on a branch, and then climbed in that close stand.

Shortly after Craig got up in his tree stand, the wind started to pick up and the camp boat crashed and banged against the shore. With all the difficulties and the time it took to row, Craig only had a short time to hunt in his stand this first evening. Fortunately, he didn't need much time, because a bear came strolling up shortly after he got there. You would think that the noise from a boat crashing against the shore might have spooked that bear away. Oddly enough the clamor seemed to distract the bear's attention away from Craig. After an excellent shot Craig made with his rifle, the bear never took another step. Not a bad start with only one afternoon invested in the trip.

The bugs did find a few openings in my mosquito netting protection though and it was hard to tell if a particular mosquito was inside or outside of my netting. This netting was annoying, uncomfortable, and I was still getting bitten. I remember thinking the next netting protection I'd buy would be different. It was also my hope that the next purchase of netting would be very soon.

Craig overcame the mosquito problem during the time he spent on his bear hunt; however, he did have one relapse. He took off his gloves to gut out the bear. The mosquitoes and black flies loved him for that. Craig's hands were so puffed up from all the bites that he could hardly even bend his fingers.

The next morning Craig slept in and didn't hear the scream. There was a meat hook in the walk-in cooler at camp. We took the big northern that a fisherman caught off the hook and hung Craig's bear on the hook. It seems that a cute child had heard there was a northern hanging on a hook in the walk-in cooler. He wanted to see the northern, strolled into the cooler, turned the corner, and was face to face with Craig's bear; thus the scream. We would make it up to the child later.

That first morning, it was time for us to try some fishing. The present warm spell had not only triggered the population explosion of the mosquitoes, but the locals had mentioned that this heat should also start moving the smallmouth bass onto the shallow spawning flats. Most of the shorelines on this lake are picturesque steep rock walls. It took a while, but when we found that first shoreline with shallow water, we knew this could be the spot.

Craig and I used the circumstances from that old TV show, The Odd Couple, to describe our personalities when confronted with different problems. Craig is more like Felix Unger (the neat, orderly, precise, and tidy person), while my traits are more like the cluttered slob, Oscar Madison. The following episode of this trip would be a prime example to show our personality differences.

After we discovered that first shallow water smallmouth spawning flat, I got excited and the adrenaline started pumping. As the boat drifted across the flat, I was running to the front of the boat to reach a potential fishing spot, then charging to the back, throwing poles and lures every which way trying to find the most effective pattern to catch any fish that might be moving in the area. My feeling was that the more casts we could get with different lures and techniques, the sooner we would discover a good fish catching pattern.

Craig is more like Felix sitting comfortably in the boat patiently and neatly trying his luck. He mentioned to me a few times that we were here to fish and asked, "Why are you running all over the boat?" He felt that I was generally destroying any semblance of order.

When I finally discovered the best lure, along with its proper retrieve, for the present fishing conditions, all calmness left the vicinity of the boat. It seems that a chug bug lure with an extremely fast, erratic, retrieve challenged any smallmouth bass in the area to search and destroy the lure. I started to catch and then release several smallmouth bass in the 17 to 19 inch class.

My patient partner Craig with the "Felix" personality finally abandoned his neatness traits and was happy to borrow my only chug bug to cash in on the action. He was rewarded with several hefty smallmouth, including the lunker of the trip, a 22" monster smallmouth bass. In fact, he really got into it, and now, as we drifted through the area, he was running to the front and then to the back of the boat, kicking lures and poles out of the way.

After awhile, I just sat back, watched him, and started laughing. Now Craig was causing the chaos and doing what he didn't want me to do. I mentioned this contradiction to him, but he didn't see the humor in it that I did. When the action finally did slow, he paused to reflect on a great time, and then he cleaned up the boat a little.

Back at camp a father and his son came up and asked us how the fishing had been. We told them, "Fantastic," and then mentioned the lure and retrieve that really turned on the fish. The kid turned out to be the same kid that got the scare from the bear in the cooler. He thought he had a lure like that and they were going to give it a try. Meanwhile, Craig and I drove to town (pulling the empty boat trailer) to see if by chance we could find a sport shop that carried "the hot lure" a chug bug. We were in luck. There was one chug bug lure right there on the shelf in the only sport shop in the town of Espanola. We couldn't believe it and Craig quickly purchased that lure. I also purchased some mosquito netting.

Before I headed out on my evening vigilance of the bear bait, our friend, that cute little kid, came back for a visit. He and his dad had tried to duplicate our success on the smallmouth, but were not as lucky. He had mustered up the courage to ask me for a little more information on those lures we had been using. I told him I could do better than that and gave him a chug bug lure.

Craig had overheard us talking and after the kid left, Craig said he was impressed with what I had done and how thoughtful it was of me giving that kid a hot fishing lure. We found out later that the kid caught a nice bass on his first cast with that lure.

On the third day of the trip, we had an unfortunate event. After trailering my boat all the way up to Canada for the trip, the top cylinder of my outboard blew a piston. This turned out to be a blessing. It cost a bundle to replace the motor; however, because the bear stands I had been hunting at were so far away, I had to save boat-travel time and hunt the stands that were closer to camp. That turned out to be a fortunate choice.

We made a trip to check the bear baits. Yet another bear had hit the bait, where Craig shot his bear. The guide said it would be a good idea to choose that close stand and just hunt there. If you hop from stand to stand, you take the chance of missing the opportunity when a bear does return. The fishing stayed good; however, the boat trip to the fishing area did eat up a lot of time. We put the 5-hp camp motor on my 17-foot Stratos Deep V fishing boat. Did you know that a 5-hp motor carrying a dead 70-hp motor and two fishermen goes less than 4 mph?

Craig was particularly ornery that next morning. It might have been because he had spent so much time cleaning out the cabin. The Felix syndrome struck again. I hadn't been too receptive about taking off my hunting boots to walk on his clean floor in the cabin. However, the more likely reason that Craig was perturbed was because he went to the truck and found out I actually had not given that kid my chug bug lure. I gave that kid Craig's chug bug lure. Those lures were a hot item and I didn't want to give mine away. I didn't care how desperate that cute kid was or how ornery Craig might get.

Some of the other bear baits had been hit by turkey vultures, and even wolves. But with the exception of a few birds and one pine marten, I had still not seen anything at my chosen bear baits.

Thursday night, Craig dropped me off at my stand with the tiny camp boat. Then he motored off with his video camera to watch the bait stand that had been hit by the wolves.

The stand I was in was a unique baiting area, because not only was there a bait close to my tree stand, but 75 yards across the bay to my left there was another bait tied on a rope and hanging high in a tripod.

Finally, after six evenings on stand, I thought I actually heard something moving close to my stand through the brush. I slowly and quietly adjusted my posture from flat on my back, staring at the clouds, to a ready position. Just as I started to imagine what this close noise could be, I heard the rope break from across the bay at the far stand.

With a quick glance, I saw him. It was a huge bear just coming back down to all fours with the bag of meat in his mouth. This excited me, not only because I finally saw a bear, but also because the camp helper had said, "If a bear can reach up and get this bait with claws, it is big enough to shoot." This bear had retrieved the bait, but not with his claws. He was so big, he could reach up to the bait with his teeth. He hit the ground running and I had only a split second to get the bear in the scope and pull the trigger. I was hoping I made a perfect killing shot, but I had two hours to ponder this thought because I had to wait for Craig to come back with the boat. Craig might even be later if he stopped to tidy up the boat.

During the longest two-hour wait in my life, I thought about the real possibility that I might soon be tracking a dangerous, wounded, very large bear into some rugged, unknown territory in the dark.

Finally Craig came putting around the bend with the tiny 12-foot camp boat. He must have heard me shoot and asked if I got a bear. I told him I didn't know, but I had a shot. "Let's get across the bay to check it out." Halfway across the bay my heart raced again because I thought I could see a big black mound in the brush.

As we approached the steep rock shoreline, I jumped out on the rock point. To be safe, Craig asked me to load my 30-06 with a few more rounds before I approached the bear. I was awestruck at the size of this thing. I walked up to the bear and as I started to roll it over, it gave out a roar. A growl from a huge black beast that you are holding onto can turn the average standing person into a streaking fool moving at blistering escape speed. I fled the scene, with my rifle in hand, in panic mode trying to discover a safe place to get me out of this perceived predicament. This safe place turned out to be behind unarmed Craig. While in panic mode, I must have remembered an important survival skill when being chased by a bear. That survival skill was I might be able to run faster than Craig.

This bear was really dead; however, because the shot had broken the bear's spine, air had been trapped in its lungs. When I rolled him over that air was forced out through the bear's vocal cords. That huge dead bear gave me an everlasting shot of bear respect. I did not, however, save my shorts to help me remember this lesson.

The next chore was to gut the bear. I remembered how Craig's hands looked after he took off his gloves to gut his bear. I also remembered I was presently wearing Craig's gloves. I mentioned to him that he was a great hunting partner and asked, "By the way, could I keep these gloves?" I was not going to take them off to do this job. It surprised us how small a gut pile there was for a bear. It has something to do with not having four stomachs like a deer.

Next we had the task of getting this approximately 300 pounds of bear into that little boat. No matter how hard we tried, we could not lift him into that boat. We finally had to put the boat in the water, tie a rope on the bear, (just in case this didn't work) and tie ropes on the tiny boat to hold it against the steep rock shore. Next we rolled that bear down the rock ledge into the boat. Thankfully it worked and the bear landed in the boat. However, the boat now sat dreadfully low in the water and after the two of us boarded, there was very little space between the gunwale of the boat and the water. Thank goodness it was a calm night. A tiny wave on the water would have gone right into our boat.

This turned out to be a very memorable trip for Oscar and Felix.

NEWTON'S LAW

When I was in college I bought a canoe. That canoe was fun to take on fishing trips with my college buddies down the local rivers. We soon learned that to catch fish it was important to anchor above good fishing spots. We were ingenious, cash-strapped students, so we tried to cobble together an anchor by tying a rope to a rock. We also attempted to make an anchor with a pail of rocks. For the record, rocks never stay tied on a rope and rocks in a pail lead to lost pails without handles or worse. Finally we decided to scrounge money out of our college book fund to buy a real anchor.

My college buddy, Jeff, and I would make the maiden voyage with our new anchor. In the first deep hole in the river, our new anchor got stuck on the bottom. In an effort to get our anchor back, we pulled so hard on the rope the canoe took on water. The anchor held tight. But, we were stubborn and would not give up our attempt to save that new anchor.

Then, because we were college boys, we thought we should try something smart. We paddled to the shore and standing there we both pulled on the rope to liberate the anchor. The anchor still proved smarter than we were. We tried our college geometry smarts and decided to change angles, so we paddled to the other shore and tried pulling again. Still we had one stuck anchor. Finally, in desperation, we got the canoe directly over this immovable anchor and decided that one of us should dive in this deep hole and get it. After a four out of seven coin toss argument, I jumped in that cold river. I took a big breath and pulled myself hand-over-hand down the anchor rope, to the ominous depths of the bottom.

If I got my hands on it I could surely dislodge that precious but obstinate anchor. After a great deal of tugging and pulling, my lungs were in dire need of fresh air. Suddenly the anchor popped loose from the rock it had been wedged under. Now all I had on my mind was to get to the surface for air, and as quickly as possible. With a burst of panic induced adrenalin enhanced energy, I pushed my feet

off the bottom and sprang up as hard and fast as I possibly could to reach the surface.

I must have skipped class and gone fishing the day the professor taught us the lesson about Newton's first law of motion. That law states, "An object that is in motion will not change velocity (including stopping) until a force acts upon it." Or more closely related to my present predicament, the canoe that was directly above me now acted as a force directly upon me. Knowledge of this Newtonian Law could have saved a very nasty bump on my head.

Jeff, the coin-toss winner, was peacefully waiting in the canoe when I was struggling below with that darn anchor. Jeff must have also skipped the lesson on Newton's Law because he was so startled when he heard the bang of my head on the bottom of the canoe he almost jumped right out. Take that for winning the coin toss, Jeff.

Signed, Lumpy

THE DOG

A long time ago, before cell phones, I went fishing with a good friend, Bert. We also took my wife's little black dog named Nikki. The place we chose to fish was Lake Poygan. Our landing was on the east shore where the Duck Inn once was.

We launched, put the dog in the boat, and then Bert tied up the boat on a dock. (Nikki had a special spot in my boat as she curled up under the steering wheel and you hardly knew she was there.)

The parking lot is a long way from the landing, so I drove off to park my vehicle with the empty trailer. It took a long time for me to walk back to the boat. A breeze over the water had kept Bert occupied keeping the boat from banging on the dock.

We fished for about six hours and had a great time. We caught eight different species of fish that day, including some walleyes and white bass and crappies that we kept for eating.

After we were done fishing, I docked the boat and took the long walk back to the vehicle. There was a note on the windshield. It said, "I have the dog back at home." Oh the dog. I did not notice that Kathy's quiet little dog had not been in our boat all day.

The dog must have jumped out of my boat when I was parking the car.

I got home and found out that the dog had spent the day jumping in and out of people's boats at the landing. Finally someone went to the Duck Inn and called our home phone number, which was etched on Nikki's collar. Kathy had driven to the landing, rescued the dog, and left the note on my windshield.

When I got home Kathy, met me at our front door. She was so angry she said, "Go straight to the doctor to get a CAT scan, because there is something wrong with your brain."

She might be right because I get so focused when I am fishing that I can become oblivious to anything that is not connected to fishing. It was a long time before I was allowed to bring Nikki along on another fishing trip. Believe me, I never forgot the dog again. And on a side note I never did get a CAT scan, because it was a dog that I lost.

LOST A BOAT

I like bow hunting, especially during the rut (mating time) of the white tailed deer. The spot chosen for this hunt was a remote undeveloped public hunting area along the Wolf River. I used my boat to reach this hunting area. After a brisk walk with a climbing tree stand on my back, I was at my hunting spot. Only a few minutes went by, when a doe being chased by three bucks came running by.

That doe stopped in an opening less than 20 yards from me and as she stood there she kept twitching her tail. I assume this twitching was to entice those bucks. The biggest, an 8-point buck with wide antlers, was next in line and closing in. I clipped my new, very sensitive back tension, released on the bowstring and drew back my bow. As the buck approached, I held my site pin in the vicinity of the doe, assuming that the buck would be entering the opening shortly.

Sure enough he came right down the same trail and entered the opening. As I started to move my site pin to the vitals of the buck, the arrow suddenly and unexpectedly released. Both the doe and the buck stood motionless at the sound of the errant arrow. I tried to quietly load another arrow, but the buck was on full alert and heard me move. He ran off and joined the other two bucks. *After about 10 minutes* the doe finally walked off still twitching her tail.

You can hunt for years to get a buck like that standing broad side in perfect bow range. Now when it finally happens, I don't have an arrow on the bowstring.

This is where the story takes a sad twist. When I retrieved that arrow out of the ground there was blood. I had inadvertently hit the doe. There was no way of knowing exactly where I hit her but hopefully the arrow just grazed her. I suspected there was a poor chance of recovering that doe, but I would give it my best effort.

I marched back to my boat and drove home to get some late night trailing help from two friends, John and Brad. Five hours later we returned to the landing and navigated my boat upriver into the darkness. We pulled up on the riverbank and started off to find what little blood there might be on the trail. (This was one of the first times I had used a

GPS and that thing was like a high tech trail of permanent breadcrumbs. It guided us on our way through the swamp and darkness.) We began our tracking adventure trudging into the eerie glow of a Coleman lantern.

After several hours of searching a faint blood trail, we had burned up the Coleman lantern fluid and decided to give up for the evening. We headed back to the boat with help from a flashlight and that GPS. We found our way back to the exact spot where the boat *had been*. Notice the "*had been*" in that statement.

The confounding events of the night must have distracted us from tying up the boat. Because of the heavy rain from the day before, the river was rising. It raised just enough to float our boat down river without us. To recap; we do not have a boat, the landing is several miles down stream on the other side of the river, and this was before cell phones were common. We wandered around along the riverbank searching for our runaway boat, passing blame from one to another. The phrases, "I thought you tied it up, no I thought you tied it up," echoed on and on into the evening.

We did not find our boat so we decided to hike downriver several miles to get across from the boat landing. When we got there, we hollered and screamed in the direction of the cabins. There was no response.

My next thought was to swim across the river, but my buddies convinced me that swimming across in water that cold could kill me.

We then decided that our only option, besides maybe smoke signals, or building a raft, would be to trudge several miles back up river. Then we would angle left through several miles of swamp. If our plan worked we should find Hwy X.

It was a long tedious chore and our GPS did not help much for finding the road. Back then you had to have been to a spot first for a GPS to be helpful. (With the newer GPS systems you can call up an aerial photo of your surroundings and head on out.) We found the road using dead reckoning and our dim and dying flashlight. We walked down the road a few miles to a, closed for the winter, campground. Hooray we found a pay phone. Of course continuing our pattern of luck for the night, no one had change to use in the pay phone.

John knew a homeowner several miles down the road. Did you notice several miles seem to be the theme for this night. We were lucky, after a few minutes of very late night door pounding, John's friend was amiable enough to allow us to use his phone. My wife, Kathy, answered the call and made the run to rescue us.

We dropped John off at his house, retrieved my truck from the boat landing and dropped Brad off at my house where he had left his truck. Even though it was cold and late, I wanted to find my boat before it drifted away into the next county. My wife put on warm clothes and I put on some warmer clothes. We then headed out for my third trip to the hunting spot.

We needed a search boat to look for the one I lost. My son, Chad, has a boat so we headed over to where it was stored and hitched it up. After thinking about our situation, we would need some light. The lantern was empty and the flashlight was almost dead. We returned to our house and picked up a spotlight. My spotlight plugs into a power point on my boat. Naturally Chad's boat does not have a power point; therefore, I had to do some late night wiring to set up his boat for a spotlight.

There is an expression I had often heard before that night but paid little attention to. That expression states: "Nothing is easy." With all the obstacles thrown our way, on this night I endorse the expression: "Nothing is easy."

Kathy and I finally made it back to the boat landing and launched Chad's boat. We carefully eased up stream using the hot-wired spotlight to scan the wooded riverbanks.

I grumbled to my wife that my boat could have drifted down to Fremont by now. As the cold wind continued whipping around us, my boat was still nowhere in sight.

We reached the spot where the boat had drifted away and I handed the spotlight to my wife. I turned the boat around, and headed back down stream. Having gone this far without seeing the boat meant one of two things. Either we missed it or that boat had gone several miles down stream and had already passed by the landing where we put in. It might very well be in Fremont before we catch up to it. Suddenly Kathy shouted "I see a reflection of something right there." We motored over and much to our delight there was the lost boat, caught up in some over hanging brush a measly 25 yards from where we originally left it.

It is a mystery how three of us could have walked within approximately 10 yards of a 17 foot boat several times without ever seeing it? We towed our newfound boat to the landing and this time secured it to shore with a rope. We put my son's boat back on the trailer and returned his boat. We returned to the landing, (my fourth time) and put my boat on the trailer. As we headed home we watched a beautiful sunrise.

I took a nap and then spent much of that day back in the swamp looking for that doe. It was unfortunate that I never did find her but that did encourage me to think she would recover.

Believe it or not I was back hunting in that same tree early the next Saturday morning. I got settled in well before daylight and waited for the sunrise. Famous Quote: *You can enjoy a sunrise only if you wait for it in the dark.* After it got light it only took a few minutes of rattling antlers together before a buck (one of the smaller bucks from before) came charging towards my tree. This time after a well-placed shot that buck got a ride home in my recently unlost boat.

I was happy and thankful to have taken this deer. Remember that big buck, the same buck that was instrumental in getting us in that predicament a few days before?

During the excitement of the smaller buck responding to the rattling antlers, that big buck had somehow silently snuck up underneath my tree. After my shot at the smaller buck, I watched in disbelief as that big 8-pointer once again bounded off to safety.

I, on the other hand, had been doing what I seem to be good at; *waiting in the dark.*

ALWAYS GREENER

I fished a tournament with my good friend, Randy Split-gerber, at Lake Wausau, Wisconsin. There happens to be a golf course along this lake and, on tournament practice day, we caught some bass under the low bridge that led into the golf course waterways. We just had a feeling that if we could somehow get under that bridge and into the golf course ponds, we would catch a bunch of fish and win this tournament.

The problem was the bridge was so low that we could not get our boat, as it was, under it. I convinced my usually more conservative partner that we should take some tools with us on tournament day. Then we would be able to remove the motor to have a lower profile. The lower profile would allow us to squeeze our boat under that bridge.

On tournament day we went straight to the bridge, took off the seats, unbolted the heavy motor, and laid it on the bottom of our boat. Then, with the enticement of catching big bass, we got on our backs and struggled to push our boat under that low bridge. Obstacles such as bird nests, spider webs, and hornet's nests did not deter us.

After that ordeal, we reached the Promised Land - the other side of the bridge. We thought we were in bass heaven. We did notice though that occasionally there would be a noisy splash in the water around us. It was usually preceded by a loud shout that sounded like "foooour." I guess it was those golfers hoping we would catch four fish or something.

Well, we didn't catch a single bass and, to rub salt in our egos, we noticed another bass boat coming towards us from the other direction! We couldn't believe it. We asked these fishermen how in the heck they got into our secret spot. They told us that this area connects up to the main lake through a little channel from the backside. Rather than taking off the motor and going under that nasty low bridge they just motored right up to the spot.

After getting into a predicament, I often come away with an unexpected and positive surprise. This time there was not much of a reward - just embarrassment, a greater respect for the value of lake maps, and some unproductive effort.

BOAT LANDING BLUES

For inexpensive and interesting entertainment, you could spend some time at a busy boat landing. Enjoy this list of boat landing related predicaments. It's unfortunate that I have played a major role in so many of them.

————————

Forgetting drain plugs in a boat is almost common - a talent at which I excel. I once went 26 miles across the Bay of Green Bay and, after we coasted to our first fishing spot, the water started bubbling up in the bottom of the boat. That was an indication I had once again forgotten the drain plug.

While in the boat, I could not reach far enough to get at the drain plug. I had to jump in the cold waters of Green Bay to find and reach the drain plug. All I found was the drain plughole.

After flapping around for 26 miles, the little cord that held the drain plug had worn away and broken off. This left us without a drain plug and a boat that was quickly turning into a 17-foot live well. It took some jerryrigging with a stick and several wraps of electrical tape to fashion a makeshift drain plug.

———————

More than once the rope holding my boat unhooked just as I was unloading my boat in the river. Off went the boat downstream and unattached. Usually friends were near with another boat to rescue mine.

Late one fall, I decided to fish for smallmouth bass on the Wolf River in Shiocton. I backed my boat into the river and, once again, that darn rope came off my boat. I watched in wonder and disbelief as my boat slowly drifted down the river. This time there was no one else around to help rescue my boat.

I started to run along the bank to catch up to my renegade boat. As I ran, I noticed that the summer cabins along the way were vacant. I started to consider the possibility that I was not going to get my boat back and I really liked that boat.

Next I thought about commandeering a boat from one of the cabins. But stealing a boat (even temporarily) in Shiocton is akin to horse thievery. It might be safer to jump in and swim to my boat.

Did you ever take off most of your clothes and jump into a river to retrieve a boat in late fall? The flaw in a plan like that is, when you jump in cold water it is very difficult to breathe. In fact when I jumped in, I was overwhelmed at how you must gasp for every breath of air.

Even though it was not very far, I had used up all of my energy just swimming to the boat and now I was weak. I struggled for what seemed like an hour before I could get my tired body over the gunwale and into the boat. I collapsed in the boat, rested for a while, went back upstream for my clothes, and went home. About a week later I read in the newspaper about someone who had a similar experience. That episode did not have a happy ending.

————————————

There is a boat launch procedure to use when fishing with a partner and a different procedure when fishing by yourself. When fishing alone, I attach one end of a rope to a loop on the front of my boat and the other end to the ratchet strap on the trailer winch. I slowly back the trailer into the water until the boat floats off the trailer. Then I gently drive forward which tightens the rope and pulls until the boat glides up on the shoreline. Next I unhook the rope from the ratchet strap and leave the boat on the shore or, if there is a dock, tie the boat off on the dock. Finally, I park, jump in the boat, and go fishing. This works great except for that one time.

I was going fishing by myself and backed my trailer into the river. Just after I floated my boat off the trailer a fisherman floated up to the landing to take his boat out. I waved at him, then drove forward and eased the bow of my boat up on the shore.

There was no dock, so I just let the boat rest on the shore. It was time to strike up a conversation with that fisherman. I have an irresistible urge to check on the luck of other fishermen. He had been very successful and was happy to share information. We had a lengthy discussion about fishing techniques. He invited me over to his boat to check out the lures he had used to catch his limit of walleyes. I was happy to have been distracted with hot, current fishing information and was now very excited to get fishing. I jumped into my truck to drive out of the landing and park. Unfortunately, I had forgotten about one very important step to properly launch my boat.

As I drove out, my truck came to an abrupt stop. I had not untied my boat from the trailer and, therefore, I pulled my boat out of the water and onto the dry apron of the launch ramp. With help from my new fishing friend, we checked for damage on my dry docked boat.

My motor had been tilted up and the transducer bracket just popped up on a hinge so fortunately there was no damage. After a struggle we pushed my boat back in the water. I have gotten to know that fisherman because of that experience and since then we have helped each other several times. Being prone to mishaps actually does have benefits.

I tried "unsuccessfully" to drive a boat on a trailer with a bow-mounted electric motor still in the water. Besides causing severe embarrassment, this will also deliver a harsh bend to the once straight shaft of an electric motor.

———————

Another time, I hit reverse before I got close enough to the dock and dumped a good friend, Tom, in the drink.

— — — — — —

One of the most consistent fishing techniques I have found over the years, is the early spring splake and brown trout bite in Green Bay by Marinette. (A splake is a cross between a brook trout and a lake trout.) Being anxious and fighting cabin fever after one long winter, I checked the Internet for the water temperature at Marinette. The temperature charts said it was 34 degrees and that was all the info *I thought* I needed to set up a fishing trip.

I made calls to my friends, Mike and Paul, and told them it was time to head up to Marinette for a spring fishing trip. It is a two-hour trip to Marinette from my hometown of New London and another hour from Mike's house in Ripon. This meant Mike had to leave very early Saturday morning so we could be fishing during the early bite.

After towing my boat and my buddies all the way to Marinette, we were flabbergasted at the landing. We got out and looked at Lake Michigan and as far as we could see there was nothing but ice! The lake was still frozen over. There we sat with a boat and a frozen lake. Oddly enough the boys were not mature enough to simply laugh off this predicament. In fact they actually *acted* as though they were upset at me for trying to get them a great fishing experience out on Lake Michigan. Those guys are sure good actors.

That day we ended up fishing in the Menominee River, which was open and we did catch a few walleyes. However, that same day there was an incident involving a huge, well over 30-inch walleye. Too bad the landing net was not ready in time and that gigantic walleye escaped after pausing on the surface to taunt us for a long moment. This lunker walleye added even more to the already bleak humor of the day.

———————

A friend told me about his first attempt at power loading his boat on a trailer. He went a short way out into the lake and got a moving start, faster than recommended. His light little flat bottom boat went temporarily onto his trailer. And then, to his surprise, it kept right on going past his trailer and into the bed of his truck. It took a moment to recover from the surprise of his first drive a boat on a trailer attempt. Several helpful fishermen picked up his boat and walked it back out of the bed of his truck and onto the trailer.

———————

I was once called to a boat landing and asked to bring my scuba gear. A fisherman was attempting to back his trailer into the water at the landing. Unfortunately, his vehicle and trailer got away from him. When I arrived at the landing, there was no vehicle or trailer in site. The owner sheepishly pointed to the river. My task was to attach the line from a tow truck to the bumper of his car that was now past the landing and 15 feet deep in the Wolf River. Imagine making this call to your wife, "I will be a little late tonight dear, my car went in the river and got a bit wet."

———————

A guy in Fremont, Wisconsin tried to launch his boat for the very first time. He did not use the normal procedure of unhooking the boat from the trailer. He unhooked the trailer from the hitch of his car and backed his boat in the water with the trailer still attached. When he realized his boat was riding very low in the water and he could hardly move it, he knew something was wrong. He nursed it back to the landing. It took four people to pull that boat/trailer combo out of the water and back on the trailer hitch of his vehicle.

———————

I have a friend, Hank, who likes to play practical jokes on his buddies while fishing. Well, his friends thought they would get back at Hank so they put axle grease all over the handle of Hank's boat winch. My friend, Paul, chose a bad time to help and grabbed the greased handle intended for

Hank. Hank thought it was pretty funny - Paul not so much. Even though Hank vehemently denies it, Paul has doubts about who actually put the grease on the winch handle.

—————————

On one attempt to get my boat and trailer out of a landing, I inadvertently backed a trailer tire into a deep underwater hole. I could not pull my trailer out of the river. I then tried four-wheel drive, but it was still stuck. I gave it even more gas and when that trailer did move it jumped like it was shot out of a cannon. I figured something must have gone wrong when that trailer pulled sideways and not behind my truck. The axle bolts on the trailer had actually pulled out through the frame of the trailer.

It was a slow drive back to my house because my truck was in one lane and the crooked boat/trailer took up the other lane. After several hours of hammering on the trailer frame and a little welding, we were back to using a single lane on the highways.

—————————

I have a friend nicknamed Red who liked to drive his boat right up on a partially floating dock. This partially floating dock happened because one of the floats under this dock had filled with water and that held the edge of the dock just under the water. This made the dock work like a ramp that he would use to drive his flat-bottom boat on. He mentioned how great this system was; "I don't even have to tie up my boat, I just drive up on this make/shift ramp and my boat will wait for me on the dock until I am ready to fish again."

It worked great except for one time. On that attempt, just as the front of his boat approached the "ramp," a wave from a passing boat lifted the edge of his ramp/dock out of the water. As you might know, the front of a flat bottom boat is square. The wave that lifted a corner of his raft out of the water turned his boat "ramp" into a boat stop! Starting from the back of his boat, Red did several unintentional forward body rolls until he finally ended up out of the boat and sprawled out on the ramp. His boat remained in the water. The witnessing fishermen in the area all started clapping and gave Red thumbs up for his incredible boat-stopping trick.

———————

Jim and I returned to the landing after a very successful day of salmon fishing on Lake Michigan. We loaded the boat on the trailer and eased up to the fish cleaning station. We were at the fish cleaning station partly to clean the fish but mostly to show off our cooler, which was full of salmon, to the other fisherman. Rather than try and lift the heavy cooler of fish out of the boat, Jim decided to jump in the boat.

When he thought some of those fishermen at the cleaning station might be looking our way, he held up our two biggest salmon. His attempt to climb out of the boat holding those two huge fish did not turn out the way he had planned. As he swung his leg over the gunwale, his pant leg got hooked on a bolt. It was a heavy-duty bolt placed there to secure a rod holder. Jim's pant leg stuck on the bolt. The weight of those fish threw him off balance and Jim's body kept on going right over the side of the boat! I heard him holler and ran to see what happened. There was Jim, still holding both fish, hanging upside down by his pant leg.

The fishermen at the cleaning station were really impressed with Jim's salmon dismount trick. One fisherman even scored him a respectable 9.

———————

A long time ago, I purchased a bright orange 14-foot boat. Unfortunately, that boat did not have a rod storage compartment. And again unfortunately, I have a very hazardous, do-it-yourself streak in me. This meant I had no choice but to build and secure a homemade rod locker to the bottom of my brand-new boat. This boat had the tri-hull design, which meant there should be plenty of room for screws to hold hinges for the homemade rod box.

Even though the interior of my boat was orange and the carpet on the new rod box was black, I was very proud. Unlike many of my projects, this one actually worked. The door opened and closed and the rods fit into the individual rod tubes that I had strategically placed in my new rod locker. If a boat designer happened upon this rod locker, they would surely desire, and maybe even patent, my ingenious design.

A few days later, word got out that the walleyes were biting. I called two people, that I thought were friends to go fishing with me. Would they be astonished when they saw my fancy new homemade rod locker. Well it turned out that the boys were stunned but for a different reason. If the walleyes were biting, we never did find out. We got to the landing and backed the boat and trailer into the river. The boat however, would not float off the trailer. This should not have been a problem. It was fairly common that a boat would not leave the trailer at a landing.

Standard practice for this situation was to check the usual culprits. Was the winch strap unhooked? Yes. Did I remove the chain by the winch? Yes. Are the tie down straps on the back of the boat removed? Yes. The boat still would not budge from the trailer. Mmm. Did the screws from my clever new rod box go through the bottom of the boat and into the trailer bunks? Darn it - a big yes!

So, to summarize, I had just discovered that my new boat had several screws protruding through the hull and into my new trailer. Plus, the walleyes were biting but, because my boat was screwed to the trailer, we couldn't even use the boat to try and catch them. You would think that "friends" would try and console you if you got yourself into a predicament like this. Not my friends, they demonstrated no concern for my feelings, in fact witnesses recalled several fishermen at the landing that day laughing profusely.

BUCK FEVER

Many hunters are susceptible to the phenomenon of buck fever. There are symptoms to look for.

A mild case of the fever might be if you squeeze the trigger of your rifle at a deer but only hear a click and no bang. This is from forgetting to load the gun, which actually is not unusual.

More severe cases of the fever have been verified. There is the hunter that is so excited when he sees a deer that he ejects all the bullets out of his rifle onto the ground without ever firing a shot.

The next case is a bit more advanced. Years ago we used recurve bows and flimsy cedar shaft arrows for deer hunting. Compound bows and carbon shaft arrows were not invented yet and hunting from a tree wasn't legal. A group of hunters in the LaCrosse, Wisconsin area would sometimes get together and drive deer. Often, when a deer would pass by and a hunter shot with those flimsy cedar shaft arrows the arrow would break as the deer ran off. These hunters had a tradition of sticking a piece of the broken arrow in the ground to mark the spot where the deer ran off. Then when the deer drive was over some of the hunters would go to the piece of broken arrow to use it as a starting point for tracking and hopefully recovering the deer.

Well, there was one hunter who, after several years, had never shot a deer. His lack of success was the direct result of the buck fever. However, getting shaky knees or forgetting to aim along with many other buck fever ailments had not deterred him. Finally on this hunt he got his reprieve, sort of. He actually hit a deer with his arrow. Remember, he had watched several hunters mark the deer exit trail with a broken piece of arrow. His deer had run off without breaking the arrow.

Now he wasn't sure what to do to mark the spot where his deer ran off. The logical idea he came up with (during this episode of buck fever) was to reach into his quiver and break a perfectly good arrow across his knee. He used a piece of that broken arrow to mark the trail where his deer ran off. That is a case of extreme buck fever.

My friends have tried to convince me that I show signs of the fever. Here is one of my typical hunts, so you be the judge. Not that long ago, I was hunting alone on our land near Tigerton, Wisconsin. It was on a Wednesday and I was lucky enough to harvest a deer with my bow and arrow.

That Thursday I was looking for something in my Ford Explorer and noticed that my bow case was empty. Darn, where was my bow. Then I remembered and made a recovery drive back up to the land. After shooting that deer, I left my bow laying out on the trail next to the food plot. As long as I was there, I could look for my lost watch (that was left at the gut pile) and maybe find an arrow I must have dropped.

Come to think of it, similar things happened to me the year before. That year after harvesting a deer, I left my bow hanging on a branch and also lost my shooting release. You know I cannot seem to keep a hunting knife very long. I suspect many of those lost knifes are on permanent watch duty at gut piles. Could this be the buck fever warning my friends keep mentioning?

Thinking way back I may have demonstrated signs of these buck fever predicaments early in my hunting career. On one opening day my friend, Mike, and I went deer hunting by Spooner, Wisconsin. We drove to our hunting spot early in the morning and headed off on our separate ways into the wilderness.

After wandering around in the dark for a short time, I got totally lost. I didn't bring a flashlight, so I couldn't see my compass and GPS wasn't invented yet. I happened upon

a tree where the top, at about 10 feet up, had broken and leaned back down to the ground. I decided to stop wandering around and climb to the top of the broken tree. I could remain there till daylight, regroup, and maybe figure out how to find my way back to the car.

I spent some time wondering how I seem to get myself in these situations when my thoughts were interrupted. Would you believe it, a buck walked by about 40 yards away? He stopped in an opening in the brush and, by golly I got him, my first buck.

After this memorable first buck experience, the standard course of action after the shot should have been to climb down the tree, tag the deer, gut it out, and then wait for my buddy Mike. Hopefully, Mike heard the shot and could find me because I was lost. There was an important and highly recommended element of the standard course of action I failed to carry out. After shooting my first buck, I did not take the time to climb out of the tree but rather jumped 10 feet down out of the tree. When you are 16 you can do stuff like that and not even get hurt - a little luck helps.

There are few thrills in a hunter's life that compare to getting your first buck. I can assure you watching your kids harvest their first deer is just as exhilarating. I can also assume that being present when the grandkids shoot their first deer will be just as memorable.

I do enjoy hunting with my boys; they are particularly helpful if I get a deer. They lend a hand by gathering up my misplaced gear and help straighten out the foolishness that happens because of my buck fever affliction. You would think that, after almost 50 years of hunting, I could get a better grip on this buck fever thing. But somebody said, "You know, if you don't get excited when you go hunting maybe you shouldn't go."

26 MINUTE TURKEYS

One afternoon Mike and I headed up to the cabin near Tigerton, Wisconsin. We had plans to hunt early Thursday morning, which was the second day of the spring turkey season.

We got to the cabin Wednesday afternoon a bit ahead of schedule. Mike decided to take his calls, turkey decoy, and chair out to the turkey tent blind before it got dark. That way he could locate the recently erected tent and he could use the light of day to help him prepare for his Thursday morning hunt.

Mike's tent was set up beyond mine - a hundred yards or so into the woods. Mike was going to walk past my blind on the way to his so I decided to walk along and get set up in my blind for the morning hunt as well. We had about an hour of hunting time remaining and on a whim, we both decided to take our shotguns just in case. Mike brought his new shotgun with a scope.

When Mike discovered the location of his tent, he yelped a note with his box call before he arrived there. To his surprise a tom turkey boomed a loud gobble right back at him. Mike figured he had just enough time to make a mad dash to his tent without being seen.

He was thrilled because the turkey was fairly close, but because he was unfamiliar with the tent he couldn't find the zippered door. He ran two panicked circles around the tent before giving up on the zipper. He finally decided to try and hide behind the tent. Mike felt concealed and gave that bird another yelp on his box call. That old tom charged to the tent in search of what he thought was a lonely hen. Mike was peeking around the tent and motionless because turkeys are great at busting hunters that move. It was fortunate for Mike that this turkey was a desperate lovesick tom.

To Mike's surprise, without making another sound on his call and without having set up a decoy, that tom went into a full strut. When the tom's tail fan was towards Mike, that tail blocked the turkey's view. That is when Mike made his move and stood up behind the tent with his scoped shotgun. He fired his shot when the tom turned back around and exposed his head. Mike not only got his turkey, he also blew a colossal hole in the top of the tent. Mike proclaimed that his new scope was the culprit for this hole.

I was startled to hear the shot, especially because Mike was only gone a few minutes. I hoped he didn't have an accidental mis-fire with his new shotgun.

Just before I heard Mike's shot, I had settled into my blind and gave one turkey yelp with my box call. After

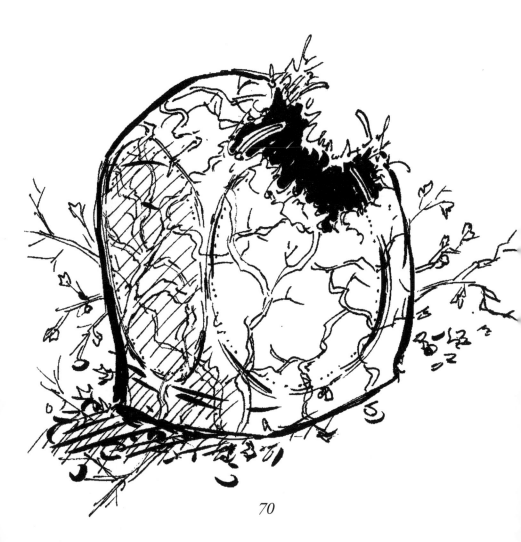

Mike's shot my instinct was to ensure Mike was all right. As I leaned back in my chair to get my phone, I caught movement of a turkey in the corner of my eye. I called Mike and whispered, "What happened?" He excitedly gasped, "I just got to the tent and shot a bird." He started to tell me the full version of the story. I abruptly whispered, "Save it for later and stay put I just saw a tom turkey and I think he is coming my way."

Five minutes later my tom was 33 yards away and Mike heard me shoot. We had tagged out with two tom turkeys in less than half an hour! Because we were tagged out we would not be able to follow our original plan to hunt in the morning. My neighbor took our picture with the two birds – unfortunately, he cut our heads off in the picture.

The hunting alarm had not been shut off so it loudly rang early the next morning. We turned it off and slept in. Even with a hole in my turkey tent, a poor picture of the hunt, and an unwarranted early alarm, we had no regrets.

ELASTIC LARGEMOUTH

My partner, Split, and I felt confident that this was a good beginning to an exciting day of fishing. We were fortunate to have already caught two keeper largemouth bass under a fallen tree at our first fishing spot. We were fishing the Northwestern Bass Tournament on Cauldron Falls. Cauldron Falls is a flowage of the Peshtigo River in the Crivitz, Wisconsin area. The shorelines belong to the power company and are without developments. Fishing there feels like being in the tranquil Canadian wilderness.

We had three keepers in the aerated live well by 9:00 a.m. and things just felt great. We had fished this same tournament several times before and previously had won with seven hefty largemouth bass, each ranging from one and one half pounds to six pounds three ounces. If we kept up the pace we were on today, we could place in the top six or maybe even win the tournament again.

We felt our spirits sag after a slow four hours, but then our luck turned sunny again with bass number four. Shortly thereafter, the tournament took on a tense, gut-level sort of feeling. At about 1:30 p.m., we eased up to that same tree where we caught that six pounder a few years before and this time that subtle tap on the line turned into a caught fish we named the "Elastic Largemouth." We would gently put him on our measuring bump board, and sometimes he would just be 12 inches and sometimes he would shrink noticeably shorter.

Registering a short fish in this tournament would be a disqualification. What would you do with a questionable fish? We placed him in the live well. We could always make what we thought would be an easy decision about keeping that fish after the tournament at the weigh-in site. There is, however, an uneasy feeling fishing in a tournament with an "elastic largemouth" in the live well.

Weigh-in time was drawing near, but there was one last beaver hut area to try before it was time to head back across the largest expanse of the lake. We didn't catch any fish at the beaver hut. It was time to leave, and Split plays the game ramrod straight. Being the cautious, conservative, calculating type, he knew the exact amount of time required to return to the weigh-in headquarters. He reached back to get the outboard started. Being on time is safe. There is no late. The word disqualified filtered through our minds. Do I gamble?

Unlike cautious Split, foolish seems to be more my style. I had to make one more cast. I launched my bait and it went into the middle of a distant brush pile, and just after the plastic worm tumbled through the brush and hit the water, a bass inhaled it. I set the hook and miracle #1 occurred. The bass came right out through the brush and I easily coaxed it into the landing net!

Split demonstrated mixed emotions. Yes, we caught another fish, but spending that time could make us late, we should have already been headed toward the weigh-in. Split has a cooler head under pressure so, as he was putting the fish in the live well and turning back to start the outboard, he forcefully said something to the effect of: "We are done fishing and are leaving now!"

Whatever it was he said, it fell on deaf ears, because by then the adrenaline that was pumping through my system had long since evaporated any sensible reasoning powers I may have had left. Split's head was turned away so he failed to see me make yet another long cast into that same brush pile.

The plastic worm again landed in the middle of the branches and somehow still managed to fall through the limbs and into the water. I felt a tug as another bass engulfed the worm. I got a good hook set, but this bass was hopelessly entangled in the brush.

Split turned as he heard me holler, "I've hooked another one!" He looked at me in disbelief. Not only was I not supposed to make another cast, now this bass had us locked to the brush pile so we couldn't leave for the weigh-in. Split started the outboard anyway and headed straight for the bass! I wound the handle on my reel as fast as a propeller on an airplane to keep up.

As the boat crashed into the brush pile, I tossed the pole toward the back of the boat. After groping down through the tree limbs and spider webs, I grabbed the line and quickly inched it through my fingers. When the fish was close enough for me to get my thumb into his mouth, I lip locked him. Then, Split cut the line at the end of the pole, as it was the only way to untangle the fish from the brush. As I was climbing back out of the brush with the bass, Split dove back for the reverse lever on the outboard. I stumbled around like a dancing clown on a string trying to stay in the boat and get a flopping bass into the bouncing live well. We only snapped off two rod tips with this experimental fish landing procedure.

We tore across the lake and entered the marked weigh-in area just as the tournament official announced the end of the tournament. We weren't late! That was miracle #3! Oh, yes, miracle #2 concerned the lower unit on my motor.

77

My partner uncharacteristically took a risky short cut over a shallow rock bar nick-named the prop adjuster and somehow the lower unit stayed on the boat.

Now after just experiencing 20 minutes of the most exciting tournament fishing my heart could stand, we had to endure the tense anticipation of the weigh-in.

Would we have enough weight? Would we have to gamble with our elastic largemouth? We mentioned our elastic largemouth to one of our tournament friends at the weigh-in. He suggested we wait until all of the other contestants had their fish weighed in. Meanwhile, we should study the fish in our live well to get our best guess at the weight without the elastic largemouth. Our friend would watch the weigh-in board and tell us the weight of the current first place. Maybe we would have enough weight and could win the tournament without gambling on that elastic bass making 12 inches. We guessed the weight of our fish to be within an ounce or two of eight pounds.

This was the day when nothing would be easy. After all the other boats weighed in, our friends told us that holding first place was a sack of fish weighing eight pounds two ounces.

So here was the dilemma. We could weigh in six fish and have a lock on at least second place and maybe even eke out first place, or we could weigh in seven fish including the elastic largemouth. With that fish, first place would either be secure for us, or if the fish didn't measure the required

12 inches, we'd be disqualified. Ugh, the dreaded word "disqualified" would penetrate our memories for years to come. What would you do in a predicament like this: take a sure second place or go for first and risk losing everything?

One more time we measured the elastic largemouth and this time he just barely, sort of, whisked the 12-inch mark. Split and I looked at each other and agreed, "How often do you get a chance to win a tournament?" We threw the elastic largemouth in the bag with the rest of the fish and headed for the weigh in scales. A tournament official bumped the first six fish, which made the 12-inch mark easily. He then reached for the elastic largemouth and positioned him on the bump board. The official had a puzzled expression on his face. He turned the fish over and checked the measurement again. As we tried to contain the swelling feelings of disaster he looked around. He then called over another tournament official.

This official bumped the fish again, and then made the decision that the fish was in fact 12 inches. We won! To this day we don't know if we would have won first place or not without using the elastic largemouth, as the fish were not weighed separately. We do know that we are thankful for fishing miracles, especially that elastic largemouth which still may be swimming in Cauldron Falls.

FISHIN' BET

I went fishing on a cold April evening with a couple of my old "friends," Dan and Mark. Dan stated he just had a feeling that, "We are going to get 'em tonight." We loaded the gear and the minnows and launched the boat south of New London by the Rawhide Boys Ranch. As we motored through the darkness downstream to the honey hole, we soon realized that it was really cold and miserable.

We took great care getting the boat anchored close to shore in just the right channel slot. After getting set up, Mark had this great idea about a fishin' bet. We all put money in the pot and Mark said and I quote, "Whoever catches the first one takes the money." Now the amount of

money was not substantial but the bragging rights - well, we are fishermen and bragging is what we are all about.

It didn't take long before I thought I was about to receive the money in the pot and more importantly all the glory. I caught a four wheeler or what is also known around these parts as a mud puppy. Mud puppies are not particularly liked because of their habit of wrapping their slimy bodies around your wrist when you attempt to take them off the hook. However, I endured and overcame this slimy creature in order to claim my prize for getting the first one. Unfortunately my friends would not pay, claiming that the first one had to be a fish. My mud puppy was considered to be an amphibian and not a fish, so I threw the mud puppy into the river and continued fishing as this drama continued to unfold.

Not long after, I caught a white bass and was relieved because I caught the first one. My two "friends" agreed that this was a fish but in unison shouted that, "It was not a walleye" and then they conferred and Mark stated that, "The bet was really about walleyes." Apparently these friendly fishing bets come with ineligible fine print.

Being more than slightly disappointed, I threw the white bass in the river and continued fishing in earnest trying to win the elusive fishin' bet - the bet which I thought I had already won twice. After an hour of wallowing in sorrow and self-pity, I caught a walleye. I was ecstatic and requested, no, at this point it was more like I demanded that they surrender the coveted prize to me. To my great dismay both fisherman agreed and announced to me, "A walleye would have to be 15 inches to qualify for this bet."

I kept this fish. However, to claim the bragging rights and respect this time I threw the "friends" in the river!

If you are looking for a fishing partner, there are two new openings in my boat.

GHOST BOAT

It was early spring, the time of the year when the walleyes run. I sauntered into the garage one morning, heading for work. As I walked past my boat, I heard a familiar noise. It was as if someone was in my boat, turning the key and trying to start the big motor, but, when I looked into the boat, there was no one there! Mysteriously, the boat engine was turning over all by itself! I was bewildered. Was a ghost haunting my boat?

I quickly jumped in the boat and twisted the ignition key, which did nothing to stop the ghost. Next I tried to pull off a wire from the battery. For future reference, a long-nose pliers and a screwdriver are not the best tools for quickly removing a battery terminal wire! It took several minutes to loosen the bolts, and, just as I lifted the wires off the battery terminal, smoke began billowing out from under the engine cover. The nauseous smoke filled the garage with the stench of burning plastic and wires.

Several hundred dollars later, after taking my boat in for repair, Boyd, my boat mechanic, told me that he didn't think it was a ghost! What he suggested is that a hole had been poked into the wire harness and water had entered through that hole. The water had corroded the wires to a point where they shorted out, causing me to believe it was some sort of ghostly being trying to start my boat. But really, what does Boyd know? He wasn't there. I was there and I am more inclined to believe the ghost theory, especially because a couple weeks later that particular "ghost" haunted me again.

Later that same summer, I took my daughter-in-law (Leslie) and her stepfather (Fran) salmon fishing on Lake Michigan out of Sturgeon Bay. This was Leslie's first trip to Lake Michigan but Fran on the other hand, is a veteran fisherman. We left New London around 2:00 a.m. (Leslie mentioned something about never being up this early unless it was closing time in a bar.)

It was a chilly, dark, and overcast morning. It also seemed a bit windy so we would keep an eye on the wind. Wind is always a serious factor when fishing on Lake Michigan. As we drove closer to our destination, I noticed two large American flags were billowing in the wind. (I like to observe those flags to determine the wind direction and velocity.) The flags were showing a strong wind but it was from the west, which meant there was an offshore wind. I assumed it would probably be tolerable for fishing, at least for a while.

We launched at Sawyer Harbor and maneuvered east through the narrow ship canal to Lake Michigan. Next we headed northeast into the darkness and, because it was an offshore wind, the lake was fairly calm. Things were looking good and I was really excited but anxious to show Leslie and Fran a good time.

However, when we were about four miles offshore, we were faced with some rough waves. Leslie was uneasy (never being on rough water or experiencing the feeling of not being able to see shore) but she seemed to be handling it. In spite of what we were all feeling none of us could anticipate what was going to happen.

We reached the fishing area in only about 20 minutes. There we shut off the big motor and started the smaller 15-hp kicker-motor intended for trolling. The kicker motor hooks up with a connecting bar to the big motor so we could continue to steer the boat with the main steering wheel. We set a northeast course to roughly follow the deep edge of the well-known fishing area called the Bank Reef.

I asked Fran to steer the boat while I set up our trolling gear. We did not realize what a task steering the boat would soon become.

We arrived at the fishing spot on the Bank Reef before light enabling us to hopefully catch the early morning bite. I set the first line in, which was a spoon pulled to depth with a small Dipsy Diver. Just as I was setting in the second line (a downrigger positioned at 60 feet with a flasher and fly), the first pole began dancing with the muscle of an early morning salmon. Leslie quickly grabbed the pole and started playing the fish. As she fought the fish, she also struggled to keep her balance in our boat. At this distance from shore, the waves were building and tossing us around.

Amidst all this excitement, she noticed the other pole and asked if that pole was supposed to be bouncing madly like it was. That line had a fish on it, also. Amazingly, there was now a salmon on each line and we had not even been fishing five minutes! The first fish was a small Chinook and was landed quickly by Leslie. She said, "That was easy enough." So I let her take over what I knew was going to be more of a challenge. This second fish was a big one and it quickly ripped out layer after layer of line off the reel's drag.

Leslie had no choice but to spend some time landing this fish and that was putting us at risk because the offshore wind was blowing us further and further from shore. The further offshore we got, the rougher the lake became. In fact, a few waves were now starting to splash over the side of our boat. With Fran's steering skills, he was able to maneuver around most of the bigger waves to minimize the splashing. But there was not a dry place left in the boat.

The second fish was a feisty Chinook salmon over the 20-pound range. After more than a 25-minute battle, we finally netted and lifted that brute of a salmon over the side of the boat. It was at that very moment, my friend "The Ghost" decided to make a repeat appearance in my boat. The big motor mysteriously lifted to the tilt-up position all by itself. This caused our boat to start spinning around uncontrollably in circles.

Fran excitedly declared that steering the boat became unexpectedly impossible. I noticed that, while there was nothing or no one touching the tilt-up switch, the motor kept on grinding in the full up position. Because the boat was now spinning around in circles it was forcing wave after wave over the side of the boat. A cloud of fear in our boat prompted Leslie to ask for and quickly be given a life jacket.

Had all the excitement of catching that big salmon put us in peril? We tried pushing and prodding all of the switches in the boat, but the motor continued grinding and was hopelessly locked in the full tilt-up position. We now had several problems to overcome before we could attempt a safe journey back to shore. The immediate and pressing problem for us to recognize was: why was this boat going in circles? In other words, how could we stop these bleeping waves from coming over the side of the boat?

When the big motor tilted up, the connecting bar between the big motor and the trolling motor wedged itself on the transom of the boat. This locked the connecting bar in place and made steering *extremely* difficult. Also, because the tilting motor jammed the connecting bar so tightly on the transom, it was impossible to remove the connecting bar.

This ghost put us in a risky predicament. The temporary solution we discovered was to have one person push sideways on the big motor and the other give extra effort on the steering wheel. This made it possible to *partially* regain control of the steering. We could not, however maintain a straight direction; we could only manage a strenuous zigzag course back towards shore. Regaining partial steering control did slightly reduce the frequency of the waves crashing over the side of our boat, but it did not happen in time for any of us to avoid being soaked to the bone.

Another big problem still existed: The big motor continued to grind to the tilt-up position, thereby draining the battery. With a drained battery we would not have power for the GPS or the ship-to-shore radio or even the now extremely important bilge pump, which was removing an immense amount of water from the bottom of our boat. We were still miles from shore and it was at this point where Leslie was confronted with a problem of her own. She exclaimed, "Where's the bathroom?" I handed her an empty coffee cup.

We had regained meager steering control but to continue fishing was now out of the question. So our new mission became - head for shore! If things became more desperate, our last hope would be to call the Coast Guard. But we then realized that calling the Coast Guard was an unlikely option. The uncontrollable tilted-up motor was draining the battery that ran the ship-to-shore radio. Since the big motor was now inoperable, we had only the power of the kicker motor for our return trip to shore. Kicker motors do not move a boat very fast and in this wounded condition, we were only able to attain crawl speed. We struggled into the ever-increasing wind, navigating a wild zigzag course. While it took only a few minutes to arrive at the Bank Reef fishing spot, it took more than two exhausting hours to finally make it back to the ship canal.

It was not over yet - this ship canal would be a challenge because it was very narrow and we could not maintain a straight line with our crippled steering. Someone besides the "ghost" must now have been looking out for us, because Kevin, a friend who guides on the lake, was also entering the canal. It had become too rough out there for Kevin to continue fishing in his much larger fully functional boat. We hollered to Kevin over the noise of the roaring wind to explain our predicament. Luckily, he gave us a tow. What a relief for our sore arms to be gently glided back through the long narrow ship canal to the landing!

Several hundred dollars later, Boyd (my frequently visited boat mechanic), tried once again to convince me that the troubles were caused by some sort of electrical problem;

water in a switch or something. However, it was rather obvious to me that once again a "ghost" had chosen to visit my boat.

Strangely enough, after numerous invitations to go fishing with me again, Leslie always seemed to be busy in some other endeavor and unable to go.

GOOD MEDICINE

It was late summer and my best friend, Mike, invited me to stay at his cabin in Michigan's Upper Peninsula - also called the UP. Besides a little trout fishing, we wanted to make a scouting trip to the woods before the upcoming deer season. Mike mentioned we should check out a new hunting area he had seen on a map.

After a full day of walking and searching the hunting land, we found some places that looked okay. However, I just didn't get that "yes this would be the perfect place" feeling. That "perfect place feeling" is important to keep you in your deer stand all day. In fact I believe one of the hardest things about deer hunting is fighting off the feeling that you should be hunting someplace else.

We were worn-out and ready to head home but there, across a huge marsh, was a thick tangled brushy area. That area just seemed to call me. The trek across the dry marsh turned out to be worth it. We located deer sign, which is what every deer hunter loves to discover. Antler rubs on trees or scrapes on the ground are great deer sign but that is not what we discovered. There were deer droppings all over the place. Finding this excrement was exhilarating; thousands of dark brown nuggets of buck hunting gold. This was the mother lode of deer sign. I picked a tree with a good view from my climbing stand and finally had that "good feeling" for next season's deer stand.

The rest of the summer, there were numerous calls and e-mails with Mike to plan for the deer season. Those communications heighten my anticipation for the hunt.

It was the 14th of November. We made the journey to the UP and I was eager and ready. Opening day would finally arrive tomorrow morning.

Early that morning, I used my GPS to maneuver back through most of the 3.4 miles of darkness to my tree. That's when I was shocked to discover that the once dry marsh I had to hike across was now flooded. I cautiously stepped into the marsh to find that the water seemed to be no more than ankle deep. I was pleased to think I was going to have clear passage across that marsh to my "good feeling" tree stand.

A dilemma occurred when I got to a channel that ran through the marsh. There was about four feet of cold dark tamarack-stained water flowing through that channel. Would this be the obstacle that would forbid my access to the good-feeling stand? My first thought was to trek all the way around this massive swamp. That might take more than an hour of tough walking through the tag alder brush around the edge of the marsh. And that encumbered detour would be in the dark. As I paused to mull over my options, a sense pulled me toward the south about 60 yards. A faint darker area appeared. I walked a little closer and that darker area turned out to be a fallen tree that spanned the channel. This wonderful tree had somehow called me and provided a path across the channel sparing me the long walk through the thick tag alders. A good feeling prevailed, because now I would be able to enjoy the sunrise sitting comfortably in my stand. This was so much better than trudging through the brush.

After completing the walk to the tree stand, I climbed the tree, and settled in with the anticipation that can only be felt by a deer hunter on opening day.

As the sun lifted the darkness, I could see much of the huge marsh. It was apparent, from my elevated position, that the downed tree I had crossed was the only safe dry passage across the water channel. This was a day that just felt right.

While contemplating my good fortune, I was distracted by a faint muffled sound. There was something moving on the crunchy snow and it was coming toward me. I could not believe what appeared. I have been hunting in the North-woods for well over 40 years and have never witnessed one of these before. A full-grown wild American bobcat walked to within 7 yards of my tree. This elusive creature reacted the way predators often do. When it got to the path I had been on, it bounded off from that path. It sensed a need to change.

This was my first year of retirement and I was also chang-ing my path. My new course led me to believe that on this day I was more a part of the Northwoods than just being in the Northwoods. As those thoughts still lingered in my head, believe it or not, a mature bald eagle completed an early morning flight, as it circled around me and landed in a tree less than 20 yards away. I have no Native Ameri-can blood in my veins, but many Native Americans believe there are signs in natural happenings. Having a downed tree call me, seeing a bobcat, and having an eagle land on a nearby branch can only mean good medicine.

A short time later, I was standing at that magical fallen tree and once again I was contemplating my good fortune. This time the fallen tree would ease my return trip. And this time it may have meant even more. I was pulling out a huge buck that entered the "good feeling spot" one final time.

BUOYS & HOOKS

I had the good fortune of meeting two very good fishing guides during the summer of 2006. One is a well-known old timer, Joe Woods. He has been fishing the Wolf River in Wisconsin for years and everybody in the area knows him. He has done well in some of the local tournaments and has also guided in the area. Joe and his son, Louis, recently set up a fishing guide association (Wolf River Outfitters). They were considering me to be one of their featured guides.

I was invited to fish with Legendary Joe. Joe's job would be to check out my fishing prowess. We met and shook hands at the boat landing next to the bridge in Fremont.

We used my boat and I was honored and nervous to meet and fish with Legendary Joe. I wanted to do my best to make a good impression. We launched the boat, slowly motored under the bridge, and headed upriver. I started in with a bad habit of mine when I am anxious. I concentrate on only one thing and that thing was talking too much.

I started shooting questions at Joe about fishing technique, Wolf River rigs, walleyes, *etc.* Joe calmly replied to my questions with only one word. The word he said was "boy." At first "boy" didn't register in my anxious head, then Joe again said, "boy." Maybe Joe was impressed with my witty thoughtful questions? Was "boy" Joe's way of saying "Very interesting?" I was thinking maybe things were looking good so far. Then Joe said, (and, this time, louder and with more purpose) "boy". But his warning was ignored as I collided my boat into a buoy, not a boy. It was a big red and white navigation buoy placed in the river. Getting myself in this embarrassing situation was not the impression I wanted to give Joe.

The other guide I met in the summer of 2006 was on the Mississippi River. I got to meet and fish with Tim Hutchinson or "Hutch" as his friends call him. Hutch is a famous fishing guide who works out of Prairie du Chien, Wisconsin. You could tell when you first met Hutch that he takes fishing the Mighty Mississippi very seriously.

I was to be the fishing guest that asked Hutch questions for a fishing show. That day Hutch gave the TV show viewers a wealth of Mississippi River fishing knowledge in spite of the curve ball I accidentally threw at him early in the taping.

The first part of the show was to cover a little-known fishing technique called "Hand Lining." This technique requires no fishing poles, but it does include a heavy chunk of lead. That chunk of lead weighs 1¼ lbs. And the lead weight is connected to a wire line that is spooled in a retractable coil.

To fish this way, you carefully drop the heavy weight with the lures attached over the side of the boat. The boat is slowly trolled forward upstream with a kicker motor. There are one or two lures (usually a rapala, shad rap, *etc*,) attached to that wire with monofilament leaders. The advantage of hand lining is the lures that you troll stay right along the bottom. You hold the wire attached to the lures by hand, thus it is called hand lining. You can feel everything on the bottom, the weeds, the sand, rocks, and subtle bites of a walleye or several other types of fish that are caught using this unusual technique.

Jeff, the producer of the show and part-time cameraman, got his camera rolling and, after a short discussion with Hutch about hand lining, we started fishing. It went well at first; I was amazed at how easy it is to feel and sense what the lures were doing when holding on to the wire that is attached to the heavy weight. The fish action came quickly on Hutch's hand-line rig. He caught a small sauger (a close relative to the walleye), I caught a sauger and then

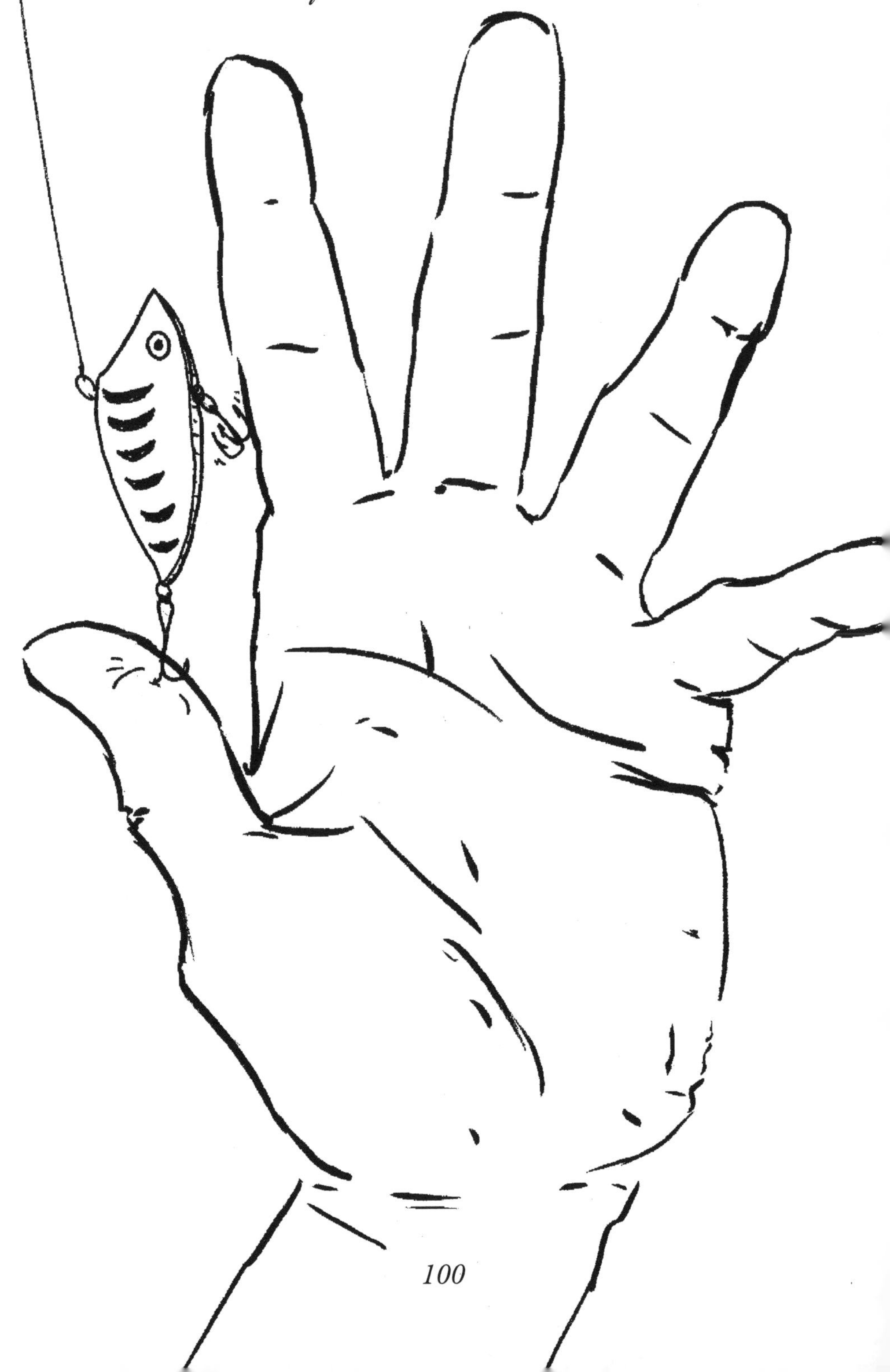

Hutch got a 20-inch walleye. Shortly after Hutch's walleye, *it happened.*

I got a lure momentarily hung on the bottom. It did pull free, but when I brought the hand-line rig up to check the lure, the back treble hook was dull. I asked Hutch for a hook file to sharpen that dull hook. He said he had one, but his file was attached to the boat with a lanyard. He told me to hand him the lure and he would sharpen the hook for me. Hutch assumed that I had taken the lure off the monofilament leader. Unfortunately, I hadn't done that. He held the lure in his hand and swung it to the sharpener. When the leader line, which I had not removed, tightened up, one of the sharp hooks penetrated Hutch's thumb. Ouch!

When you are fishing, getting a hook in a finger or thumb or some other part of your anatomy is not that uncommon.

Here is where I unintentionally added more drama to the situation. Hutch casually mentioned that he had a hook in his thumb and showed it to me.

When he showed me that hook, piercing deep into his thumb, I leaped up to assist the impaled Hutch, the same Hutch I had been trying to positively impress on our very first show with him. When I jumped up to resolve the predicament, I made matters worse. I bumped the 1¼ lb. lead weight with my knee. That knocked the weight back into the Mississippi River. That lead weight was the same weight that was attached to the leader, that was attached to the lure, that was stuck in Hutch's thumb! Ouch again! Hutch was one tough old bird. To my amazement he did not holler but casually waited for me to lift that weight back out of the river and take the pressure off his thumb.

I have lots of hook removal experience and told Hutch to hold still while I pulled the hook out of his thumb. I reached for the ever-present rusty boat pliers. Fortunately, the hook popped free with one well-aimed tug. Jeff did not roll the camera during this fiasco, but it might have made interesting viewing.

It turned out that I did get the fishing guide job at old Joes' Outfitter Shop and we did produce a good show about fishing the Mississippi with Hutch. Incidentally, whenever I have seen Hutch since that day of the hand-lining adventure he gives me a "thumbs up." But it seems to be more of a reminder about something than that of a friendly greeting.

––––––––––

Hook removal is a common topic among fishing communities. It takes only one story about a fisherman being punctured by a hook to set off a flood of stories. Every successive storyteller includes larger hooks or longer trips to the emergency room to improve on the last story told.

The most common items in a hook-removal story entails a pair of rusty pliers followed by a hard tug. The next most common story involves a pair of rusty pliers followed by several hard tugs. There was a sportswriter in my boat that will verify my expertise using a rusty pliers and the several hard tugs technique. Finally, there has been a more recent trend adopted by some hook removers. These hook removers try to push the point of the hook all the way through and then cut off the barbed point with a rusty pliers. Granted, if the hook does get pushed all the way through and the barb is cut off, the remainder of the hook removal procedure is somewhat painless for the victim.

CAUTION: If said hook remover fails in an attempt to push the hook all the way through, the hook remover who botched the job may suffer from a not-so-painless black eye from said victim.

HORSE FLIES

Many lakes are formed because of a dam. The rivers that fill those lakes are called feeder rivers. I was told that, in late summer, bass sometimes migrate up these feeder rivers because of the cooler oxygenated water. The Clintonville Pond lies 16 miles north of my home and it has a feeder river called the Pigeon River. Jumping into a new adventure, sometimes without enough preparation, is a dangerous trait of mine even though this trip seemed very innocent. I decided to test the theory of bass moving out of the Clintonville Pond and up into that feeder river.

I had never fished this river, but I had caught several bass in the Clintonville Pond during the spring. If those bass migrated into the Pigeon River, concentrating there, it could certainly be fun catching them. Would there be bass in that river this summer? One hot day in August, I planned a fishing trip to find out. I packed a little bit of fishing gear. Then I loaded my sturdy 16-foot canoe on top of my car. Planning a float trip takes a bit of maneuvering and some help. My father-in-law used his station wagon and was the helper for this trip. A trip I will never forget.

The spot I chose to begin this excursion was at a bridge a few miles upstream from the Clintonville Pond where I dropped off my canoe. My father-in-law followed me with his vehicle and we drove to the dam where I would pull out at the end of the trip. I left my car at the dam. I jumped in with my father-in-law and we drove back to my canoe at the bridge.

I have made several other trips in this canoe. When floating rivers, I often bring a heavy car battery and an electric motor to guide and position my canoe. This makes it possible to put down the canoe paddle and spend more time fishing. It looked like the water that day was a little low and too shallow for the electric motor to work. I decided to leave the motor and heavy battery in the car.

My father-in-law helped me unload and, when I thought I was ready, he waved as he headed home in his car. Boy I was really not ready for what happened.

A few annoying horseflies greeted me as I dragged the canoe through the tall grass and into the wooded area beside the river. My anticipation of catching those bass was a distraction from the bothersome horseflies. The original plan was to peacefully drift downstream and fish for the bass that hopefully would be as plentiful as the spots on a fawn. As I floated into the realm of this shaded river, the horseflies were no longer only bothersome, but they began to swarm me and became infuriatingly relentless. I swatted and swiped at them but it seemed the more commotion I made, the more flies it attracted.

I did not wear shorts, which turned out to be one of the few good choices I would make on this trip. The shirt I had on was a thread bare T-shirt with huge holes in the belly. On past fishing trips, when I carried the heavy car battery, it would rest against my belly. My wife and I wondered why I had holes in the belly of so many shirts. Finally after destroying several shirts, we realized that battery acid was slowly dissolving my clothes. I did not want to destroy any more shirts so I made what turned out to be a very poor decision. I wore one of the worn out T-shirts with the holes. That left more skin exposed for the tenacious flies.

Every square inch of my exposed skin turned into a horse fly target and was under constant attack. If I was not fast enough on the swat, I was bitten. Each bite became an extremely painful welt that lasted for more than an hour. With my father-in-law now long gone, I was left alone to fend off these tormenting flies.

Any levelheaded thinking on my part was side-tracked because of the distraction of the tormenting hordes of flies. I had a paddle and a canoe but not enough good judgment to do the smart thing. All I could think of was paddle my canoe to the pull-out at the dam. I tried paddling quickly, unrealistically thinking that maybe if I moved fast enough, the flies would not catch me. It was worthless to try and fish because I would be bitten whenever I took the time to reach for my fishing pole. I tried to simultaneously paddle and swat at the flies before they added yet another painful welt to me. This ingenious plan did not work either. I was literally, up a creek with a useless paddle. Pure desperation took over. I just couldn't take it any more and I jumped into the river. The cool water temporarily relieved the sting of the fly bites. Unfortunately, when I lifted my head above water to breathe it only took seconds for the flies to find me. I would need scuba gear for this plan to work.

Next a more primal survival instinct kicked in. I did not have any extra clothes to cover my skin. What could I use to protect myself? I went to the edge of the river and scooped out the gooiest, slimiest, stickiest mud I could dig up and slabbed it all over. I covered my face, arms, neck, and, especially, belly. It wasn't pretty but self-preservation trumps good looks. The plan worked as long as the mud was thick and I moved very slowly. Moving fast would shake off my precious coat of mud. I learned quickly how to gently paddle with no sudden movements. Here was yet another predicament, if a bit of mud slipped off, an area of skin was uncovered. When a fly would tear into that uncovered skin, the impulse to swat that fly would

be overwhelming. When I swatted, mud would fly off, exposing more skin, and thus more bites. Soon I would jump back in the river and start again with another application of mud. This whole situation was aggravated by the fact that this tiny river must not have been floated for years. Every so often a brush pile or entire tree would have to be maneuvered through or portaged around. If you want a challenge, put thick mud on your face and arms, then try to pull a canoe through thick brush without losing any of the precious goo.

After a couple of unbearable hours, I finally reached the open lake. The horse flies suddenly disappeared. It seems they do not like direct sunlight. There were people boating and fishing on the lake as though nothing had happened. I do, however, remember getting some strange looks.

I take pride in the fact that when I go fishing, I can usually find a way to catch fish. I did not find a way to catch a single fish this trip. In fact, I never even made a cast. The pain from the first few bites was beginning to subside and, in another hour or so, the pain from hundreds of other bites would be gone. Now I was as relaxed and relieved as I could have been in the last few hours. Or was I? Later I devised an almost painless plan, which, if utilized in a similar situation, would save a great deal of agony. I must confess that it took a while after the fact when this brilliant idea dawned on me. Next time I am not prepared for a horde of horseflies, I will not panic like I did last time. This time I will paddle back up to the put-in spot, by the bridge. I will leave the canoe there and head for the road. A road that is showered in glorious sunlight. Then cheerfully walk down that road to my car by the dam.

On a side note, in hot weather I have seen deer inexplicably run out of the woods and into a field jumping and kicking. Now I understand why they do that and sympathize with them.

LESSON IN THE CLASSROOM

I taught middle school for 30 years. It took me a few years of trying before I caught on to teaching. When I finally caught on, I found out I loved teaching. Catching on was as simple as spending time listening to the kids and learning a little classroom management. I wish that would have been taught in college.

Some kids responded to my passion for the outdoors and even my sense of humor. It also turned out that those kids were wittier than I ever imagined.

My teaching was done in a shop class. As an incentive for getting the shop cleaned up on time, I would either give the class riddles to solve or sometimes tell hunting or fishing stories. The girls in class usually acted as though they were not impressed with my stories, but I could see that they would usually listen.

One day toward the end of class, I told the kids one of my hunting stories. I even drew the scene on the blackboard. It pictured the swamp, the deer trails, the oak ridge where my tree stand was, *etc.* Finally at the end of my story, a girl asked if she could borrow the chalk.

I suspiciously relinquished the chalk and stood aside. She drew several boxes and rectangles on the board and then double lines connecting them.

She turned, looked at the class, and began telling her story. As she pointed to the box drawn at the right side of the chalkboard, she stated that last Saturday she and her mom started right there at the shoe store. The double lines she drew illustrated the road that they followed to her next stop, which was a dress shop. After pointing to a few more stores and describing a few of their purchases, she handed me the chalk, gave a slight bow to the class, and sat down. The class laughed and cheered.

I have to admit I started giving a few more riddles and a few less hunting stories. I am retired from teaching now, but I really do miss these kids.

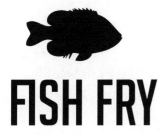

FISH FRY

For years we stayed for a week's vacation with three other couples at a resort on Lake Minocqua. The Minocqua area in Wisconsin is a good choice because it can accommodate the 4-wheelers, the golfers, the shoppers, the restaurant connoisseurs, and the fishermen of our crew. The women plan this trip for an entire year, fine-tuning almost every detail including meals and activities. Some even plan what they will wear on every day of the week. We guys know not to challenge the plan, instead just stick to it.

The plan for Thursday was for me to do a fish fry for the entire crew. Strangely, the women decided they wanted to catch the fish for this fish fry.

Before our vacation and in preparation for this fish fry, I rigged several poles for the ladies to use for catching pan fish. I also stayed up late at night during rainstorms to pick the nightcrawlers. I consulted with several fishing friends to discover good spots to catch pan fish on our lake as I rarely fish for bluegills. I wrote up a few fishing maps and plugged some spots into my GPS my friends told me about.

When packing for the trip the guys brought up the big propane fryer, the heavy-duty kettles, the special seasoning, and the expensive cooking oil. The first day of our vacation I went scouting on the lake to check out all the fishing spots my friends had told me about. We needed to make sure we found the right spot, because if we did not catch fish Thursday we would not be following the plan.

I spent a few hours and went pre-fishing to check out several of the spots. Fortunately, one spot was loaded with blue gills. Unfortunately, I found the fish deeper in the water than I had hoped and therefore I had to rerig all the pan fish poles with slip bobbers. This slip bobber fishing is a real time-consuming pain to rig up but a good way to get the ladies fishing deep enough to catch those scrappy eaters.

The day finally came for the big fishing outing and fish fry. I got all the women on a pontoon boat and we set out on our journey. We tossed in the anchor by our hot spot and the fish cooperated. Some women would touch fish, but not worms. Some would touch worms, but not fish. Some, my wife as an example, would not touch anything related to fishing except a pole, which included a weed that might be stuck on a hook. After a couple hours of untangling lines, baiting hooks, and taking fish off the hook, we had enough fish for the fish fry.

Somehow it was now my job to spend a considerable amount of time cleaning all these fish, even though some fish were on the small side. Finally, after working up an appetite, the group was hungry. The plan was frying fish.

I spent a large amount of time preparing for this fish fry. However, after rigging the poles, staying up late at night in the rain getting the nightcrawlers, tapping all my friends for information on where to catch pan fish in this lake, packing all the cooking supplies, scouting the lake to find the fish, re-rigging all the poles, untangling a hundred fishing lines, the women decided that rather than fry the fish, everyone would go out for pizza. Would we men give in to this untimely and absurd request? This was not the plan. We should stand our ground just once. I know what you're thinking, "Good luck with that."

Their pizza place of choice was the jam-packed pizza joint that always has at least an hour wait. Well, this night it turned out that the wait was unusually long. The women stayed there and sent me to find another pizza place and get a reservation. I drove all over, found another place to eat and got us a couple tables. I went back to the original pizza place to get them but then they decided they wanted to stay where they were and waited another hour or so. I went back to cancel the reservations. We waited there at least another hour and then I quietly ate the delicious pepperoni and onion pizza. No anchovies though, as some fish can leave a funny taste.

FUNNY NOISE & DONNY

Coming back from a hunting trip with long-time friend, Jim, we noticed a funny noise coming from somewhere in the front of Jim's 4-wheel drive vehicle. Naturally, we felt the easiest and best way to locate this funny noise was for Jim to climb up and ride along on the hood of the vehicle. I would drive slowly down the road; this would give Jim a chance to locate the noise.

We started out this adventure just fine. (You know those repair shops can charge a fortune to find funny noises.) Then Jim raised his hand and I assumed that meant he wanted me to stop. Suddenly Jim was gone.

We never did find that funny noise and for some reason Jim didn't think the noise was all that funny after all.

————————

I have another friend, Donny. He has special timing mixed into his personality. Donny was in a bass fishing tournament where you draw a partner. The fisherman he drew turned out to be blind. Therefore, Donny was to be ever alert and occasionally call out to his blind partner, to let him know how far away the shore was. He also told him about the stumps and weeds to more or less keep the blind guy in the fishing game. As the two were casting along the shoreline, Donny used his electric motor and moved the boat slowly along.

Around the next bend, a road came very close to the edge of the lake. After making the turn, the wind picked up and pushed their boat a little closer to the shore. As it happened, just then a car came along. Also, because of a wind gust, the blind man made a cast that was a little longer than usual. The blind guy's lure hit the car and line screamed off his reel. The blind guy was dumfounded and exclaimed, "What in the heck was that?" Donny calmly stated, "I think it was a Buick."

————————

On another fishing excursion, this same Donny was fishing *by himself* on the North end of Partridge Lake. The north side of Partridge Lake does not have a cottage, house, cabin, dock, or much of anything man made within about a mile. There is nothing but muskrats, ducks and cattails. It was a calm day and as he made a cast into the still waters of the lake, a voice asks Donny, "How are they biting?" He looks all around and *there is no one around!* God? He recalls the line from the old TV show, Sanford and Son, where old man Sanford holds his chest and cries, "I'm having the big one Elizabeth; I'll be with you soon."

Again a voice speaks saying, "Hey, how are they biting?" Donny is in disbelief as he looks again and there is still no one anywhere. Someone speaks a third time and this time it is louder, "Hey up here." To Donny's surprise and relief it was someone in a hot air balloon that had silently drifted close to and directly above him.

FLY THE WOLF
{THE TRIPLE FLY RIG}

Below is a bonus story that has been in several newspapers and a sporting magazine. It describes a fish catching technique that has helped my clients catch hundreds of fish in the last few years. Imagine the predicaments you can get into when catching up to three fish at a time.

———————

One day a friend and I were fishing off a dock on the Wolf River in New London. We watched some Asian fishermen on the bank across the river; they were catching walleye after walleye and I was fascinated. As we watched, we could tell they were not using minnows or plastic, and they could cast whatever it was they were using, a very long distance. Later we found one of their rigs stuck in a dock on our side of the river. So, at last, we got a good look at their set-up. It looked like a modified Wolf River rig. The business end of the rig (hook end) was tied with a colored deer hair fly without much hair wrapped to the hook. It was tied to a long monofilament leader and a heavy sinker.

My buddy, Steve, and I tried to figure out their technique and how to use this unconventional fishing set up. After experimenting with several retrieves, different leader lengths, line types, flies per line, and weights, we started catching walleyes.

We quickly found that this technique is effective and one aggressive way to catch walleyes, white bass and other types of fish. I believe at times on the Wolf River, it really works better than anything else I know.

Now I'm hooked on the triple fly rig.

This method will entice the same amount of strikes as the other more common methods of fishing.

Techniques such as jigging, casting, and long lining are just some of the mainstays, but make room for the flies.

The advantages of the multiple fly rig come in two ways. First, the long cast enables you to cover an enormous amount of water relatively fast and methodically. Secondly, you get an extremely high percentage of hookups to bites.

I believe the high hook up percentage happens because, the hook is on a long unencumbered drifting line, not a restrictive lead head jig. Keep in mind, there is nothing except a bit of hair on the hook of a fly so the fish can easily and naturally engulf the hook. Often I use flies with different colors on my three fly rigs, giving the fish a choice.

I do not hold a lot of stock in the color idea but, sometimes color of the flies seems to make a difference if only for the confidence of the fisherman. There is a direct correlation between confidence and success in the world of fishing.

Often times with many other fishing techniques, fishermen do not detect subtle bites, however, because of the fast cadence of the fly rig retrieve and the lightweight unencumbered hook, fish are often automatically hooked. In fact, the fish are hooked so well I usually, swing the hooked wiggling prize into the boat without the use of a net and almost never lose a fish. If the fish is over about 20 inches use a net.

The long cast of this technique keeps you undetected and away from the fish. If you are using a standard drift-jigging technique, chances are you are running an electric motor directly over the fish. Especially in shallow water this motor noise can and often will spook your school of fish.

For me, the most common use of this rig is to cast across the current. Keep a tight line and, when you feel the sinker hit the bottom, immediately rip the tip of the rod back about two feet. Allow a second or two for the sinker to hit the bottom again and, as you drop the rod tip, wind up the slack. Now snap your rod tip back about two feet again. Try to get into a cadence, and make sure you feel the bottom after the pause *every time.*

The most common problem fisherman have when they start out is pulling the rod tip back too slowly and too far back. It should be a quick short snap that should tire you out.

Feeling the bottom becomes more difficult as the rig approaches the boat and then it requires more concentration. It is a good idea, when learning this cadence, to simply reel in when the rig approaches the boat. I've noticed that feeling the bottom every time is difficult for many fishermen. However, to emphasize this point, it is important to feel the bottom every time. It will make detecting strikes easier and keep your rig from snagging on the bottom.

Another peculiarity about this technique that I've noticed happened a few times when I guided a pontoon boat full of fisherman. The fishermen that did not have slack line on their retrieve always caught more fish. So when you snap the pole, reel up quickly so there is no slack line.

For equipment I use a spinning rod at least 7½ feet long or longer. This makes the long leader more manageable. I use 10-pound braid for the main line. The long casts can create a big bow in your line, which will decrease the feel of your sinker touching the bottom. However, the fine diameter of the braided line cuts through the water easily. This improves diagnosing the subtle contact of the bottom.

I like crystal Fireline or the new orange Fireline because you can sometimes see and most importantly (as stressed before) feel the bottom. If you use monofilament on your main line, you would not be able to have this control. The mono stretches like a rubber band which can make feeling the bottom difficult.

I use a long 10-pound test fluorocarbon leader to attach the flies. See diagram below. The leader is about 65 inches long, and is usually tied with three flies. The first fly is half-way on the leader and the middle fly is halfway between the first fly and the end of the line away from the swivel. I use a palamar knot to connect the flies, but do not cut off the end of the line after tying. I leave it long and use the same length of leader line to tie all the flies.

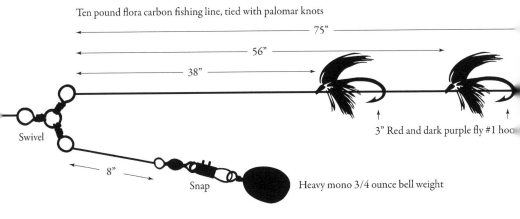

Ten pound flora carbon fishing line, tied with palomar knots

75"

56"

38"

Swivel

3" Red and dark purple fly #1 hoo

8"

Snap

Heavy mono 3/4 ounce bell weight

I use a short, 20-pound test line above the sinker and tie it about eight inches long. The heavy line makes it easier if things need to be untangled. It's important to use a snap above the sinker so the weight can be changed to match the conditions. To start with, a ¾-ounce bell sinker is a good all-around weight. If you are in a snag filled area you might try the pencil weights to reduce hang-ups. I find you need slightly heavier pencil weights to have the same feel as the bell sinkers. The weight you use depends on the water depth, current, and the aggressiveness of the fish. Keep a plastic jar with several different size weights handy.

This system has versatile uses: It will work from shore, drifting in a boat downstream, trolling, and anchoring. Clean river bottoms, holes, or clam beds are very good places to try. I have even anchored and cast straight down-river into deep holes on occasion, but this is more effective if you find a current edge where the main current meets slack water.

Trolling a triple rig like this in places like the Butte des Morts Bridge or the Winneconne Bridge is effective all summer long. We have had 20-walleye days and coolers full of white bass. During the warm water time of the year, fish are more aggressive so use heavier weights. Also, keep moving and ripping that rig when trolling forward. I like to use a heavy-action pole during the summer; it gives more snap in the rig as you rip it off the bottom. While trolling in Lake Poygan, we pulled this rig right behind the boat and picked up extra white bass while the crank baits on the boards were picking up walleyes.

It amazes me how many fish this system catches. Once, while standing on a dock with boats all around, it took only 45 minutes to catch a limit of big female walleyes. One summer, a huge school of smaller-sized smallmouth bass moved in on a flat. Four times we had doubles (two fish on the same line) of those scrappy fish. One fall there was a stretch where, eight times in a row, we were able to catch a limit of walleyes on the flies. Several of the fishermen with me that fall had no fishing experience. We even had a few incidents where we actually caught doubles on walleyes. Once, in a low-key walleye fishing derby, my partner got a 27-inch walleye on a triple-fly rig. We won.

When the white bass move in, the fun really begins. As shown in the diagram, I use the rig with three flies on the line. Getting doubles and even triples is not uncommon. I once found an extremely aggressive school of white bass and caught 11 white bass on four casts. The trick to getting doubles and triples on white bass is to let the first fish you hook swim around a bit. That will drag the remaining flies close to other aggressive fish in the school.

I use this system frequently because of its advantages, but I have experienced a few drawbacks. At least for me the rig is not as effective when the water temp is around 45 degrees or below. (There is an alternative cold-water fly and jig method that has been working very well, contact me at wilfish.com for information on this cold water technique.) This triple rig can also be a bit cumbersome to cast because of the extremely long leader, and, if it's windy, there can be some awful tangles when using three flies. Then you might limit the rig to one fly. With a triple rig, when you do snag up, you lose a lot of equipment.

Regardless, I love this type of fishing so much I've learned to live with the drawbacks and I tie my own rigs to save on the cost.

It is tricky to explain how to use this rig; however, spending about a half-hour in the boat with someone who has experience can shorten up the learning curve. This technique will also make sure you will have a lot of practice cleaning fish.

"Daylight in the swamp!"

— Logging & huntiung wake up call

Acknowledgments

Thanks to the many people that helped make this book come together. Of course the poor chaps (unnamed and named) in the stories who unwittingly happened to be on these aforementioned adventures deserve credit. My son, Chad, for the use of his boat at a crucial time. Also thanks to these invaluable folks for helping with the editing and rewrites; Brent Frankenhoff, Bob Witczak, Ginger Landers, John Faucher, Kathy Williams, Kim Jordan, Kristin Beebe, and Shawn Williams. Thank you to my 9th grade English teacher Mrs. (name withheld) who tried to convince me I was a horrible reader and writer. She was the impetus for me attempting to write this book. Even though she was probably correct, I hope she at least notices that I used fancy words like aforementioned and impetus. A special thanks to Kathy, my wife, for hearing me conveniently say, "I can't help with the dishes right now, I am working on the book." Finally I'm especially grateful to my son, Shawn, who actually jumped at the idea of illustrating and publishing another book.

Author

Randy Williams lives in New London, Wisconsin. He has long been committed to conservation and outdoor recreation. Randy has an Associate Degree in Conservation, is a certified scuba diver, a licensed fishing guide, and a taxidermist with more than 30 years experience. He is or has been a member of: The Clintonville Fishing Club, Menomonie Bassmasters, Waupaca Bass Club, The Wolf River Bass Club, Spoonpluggers, Walleyes for Tomorrow, and The Wolf River Sturgeon Trail. He also maintains ties with: The Turkey Federation, Whitetails Unlimited, Shadows on the Wolf, and Ducks Unlimited.

Over the years he has won more than 40 fishing tournaments and has spent five years as a co-host on an outdoor TV fishing and hunting show called No Excuses. He has also been an outdoor columnist for The Waupaca County Post. He still works on promotional videos for hunting and fishing outfitters. Presently, he holds the record for the most fish species caught in the Wisconsin Natural Resources magazine for the multiple species category. His total is now 67 different species of freshwater fish caught.

For 30 years, Randy shared much of his knowledge of the outdoors with his students in his general shop class for the New London School District. His student's projects often included making fishing lures, turkey calls, deer stands, etc. He is now retired from teaching and enjoys fishing and hunting full time, often with his two sons, Shawn and Chad.

The sign on his front door states "A fisherman and the catch of his life live here." Kathy, his wife of more than 36 years, picked out the sign.

Randy has a great way of putting his outdoor experiences into words. Reading this book is like being there with him on his adventures.

— *Steve Jordan*
Wisconsin NWTF Outdoor Writer of the Year

Randy Williams, an avid Wisconsin outdoors man, has accumulated countless humorous anecdotes. This collection of tales centered on Randy's passion for spending time with family and friends in the outdoor world rekindled many fond memories of my own adventures as a sportsman and I am sure it will do the same for you.

— *Mike Troyer*

Yup, I have been in many a predicament with Randy and I keep coming back for more. A unique quality that Randy has (as evidenced in this book) is that he can laugh at himself. Don't let his "predicaments" fool you. The author is a gifted hunter and fisherman. More importantly he is a good steward of our land. Everyone should have a hunting and fishing partner like Randy. Enjoy the book.

— *Paul Drzewiecki*

I've had the chance to know Randy as a friend and fellow hunter. Reading his book with stories based on predicaments he's gotten himself into as a fisherman and hunter made me laugh over and over again. I have never met as outdoorsman who gets more excited than Randy about landing a fish or making a good shot at an animal. I had the pleasure of being with Randy in Colorado when he shot his first elk. Being a part of his childlike excitement made me appreciate our hunting trip even more. Any person who enjoys hunting and fishing and just being entertained will find this book a joy to read.

— *Kim Jordan*

WWW.WILFISH.COM

Made in the USA
Lexington, KY
12 May 2014